50 Years of Years of HOT ROD

From the Editors of *Hot Rod* Magazine

MBI Publishing Company

First published in 1998 by MBI Publishing Company, 729 Prospect Avenue, PO Box 1, Osceola, WI 54020-0001 USA

MBI Publishing Company books are also available at discounts in bulk quantity for industrial or sales-promotional use. For details write to Special Sales Manager at Motorbooks International Wholesalers & Distributors, 729 Prospect Avenue, PO Box 1, Osceola, WI 54020-0001 USA.

Library of Congress Cataloging-in Publication Data

50 years of Hot rod / from the editors of Petersen's Hot rod magazine.
        p.   cm.
        Includes index.
        ISBN 0-7603-0575-7 (hardcover : alk. paper)
        1. Hot rod magazine. 2. Hot rods-- History. I. Hot rod magazine.
        TL236.3.A14   1998
        796.72--dc21   98-34423

On the front cover: Cover illustration © 1998, Tom Fritz. Legendary artist Tom Fritz created this special, nostalgic hot rodding scene to commemorate *Hot Rod* Magazine's 50-year milestone. Signed lithographs of Fritz's work can be purchased by calling (213-782-2923).

On the frontispiece: In 1984, Kenny Bernstein's new, nitro-engined Budweiser King Funny Car demonstrated some of its power for *Hot Rod*. Each blast down the quarter-mile cost the team more than $2,500 in fuel, tires, engine parts and other non-reusable components.

On the title page: Painted flames and hot rods have always been a natural combination. The cover of the March 1979 issue featured three outrageous examples: Terry Berzenye's 465-horsepower Boss 351-powered three-hole Deuce, *Hot Rod*'s very own 1970 Plymouth Road Runner, and Mel and Kathy Jeffries' immaculate 1955 Chevy Nomad.

On the back cover, top right: Hot rods and teenagers have been crucial elements in some of Hollywood's favorite story lines. In the 1961 low-budget teen classic, *The Choppers*, Arch Hall, Jr. played the rich-boy leader of a gang who specialized in stripping cars and then selling the parts to a disreputable junk yard. **top left:** *Hot Rod* photographed Jack McDermott's 1929 Ford, on 1932 rails, for the cover of the December 1953 issue. **bottom:** "The flashier the mods, the hotter the rods!" Nothing could be truer to describe Matt and Debbie Hay's twice-blown Bird on an Alston chassis. Boost was provided to two B&M blowers mounted side-by-side ahead of the motor. A pair of Mikuni 44-millimeter carbs fed fuel to the blowers, while copious amounts of nitrous oxide were pumped into the B&M manifold. It was worth the effort. Matt and Debbie picked up the Street Machine Nationals Pro Street Award in DuQuoin, Illinois in 1987.

Edited by John Adams-Graf
Designed by Katie L. Sonmor

Printed in Hong Kong through World Print, Ltd.

CONTENTS

FOREWORD
by John Dianna

Much has been written about *Hot Rod Magazine*'s 50th An-niversary. Not unlike a number of hot rodding historians, the magazine's staff, both past and present, has varied recollections concerning the history and evolution of the magazine and the sport over these past 50 years.

It seems that history, ours included, will forever be dependent upon those responsible for the chronicling of events. To some of our scribes, an event could be defined as a great day at the races. To others, it might be a late-night bench session with a luminary car builder, drinking beers at the Power Tour stops with readers, bulldozing the back-forty with one of NASCAR's greatest, or witnessing Wally Parks cut the ribbon at the new NHRA museum. To this day, some historians claim that there is nothing like enduring the sun-soaked thrill of strapping both legs and body in and about a lakester and joining some exclusive mph club. To some of us, an event can be described as a side-splitting chat with founder Bob Petersen (Pete), listening intently as he spins historical yarns about collecting advertising payments in the form of home-cooked meals.

One thing that history of the high-performance industry teaches us—a history in which *Hot Rod* has played a most significant role—is that it's about far more than the fabulous cars or the trends that many of these vehicles created. It's about more than the sanctioning bodies responsible for bringing safety, along with national television coverage and racing heroes to our sport, and it's about more than the uniquely

specialized parts and accessories that allow all young enthusiasts to create a dream. Our history is really about the unique *individuals* responsible for all this.

The story doesn't begin in 1948 with the launch of *Hot Rod* magazine. No, it

This multiple exposure of Charlie Allen's Dodge Dart funny car taken shows the simple construction of an early funny car. For more than half of a century, *Hot Rod* Magazine has provided fun, facts and how-to's to generations of auto enthusiasts.

started decades before, when enterprising young men used only the bare essentials to construct faster hot rods. Handmade components and all sorts of spindly creations made their way to the dry lakes, wooden-planked racing tracks, and the sandy beaches of Daytona to see firsthand who

was the king for the day. Today, computer-designed, 320-mile per hour top fuelers truly live up to their original moniker of "slingshot dragsters." Certainly times are different from the T-shirt-clad days of El Mirage, but can you fathom the sensation of what it must be like to accelerate straight to 320 miles per hour in 4 1/2 seconds, or even worse, to make some driving correction at that speed? That takes a certain unique *character*.

Historians are fond of portraying the notion that gatherings at such places as El Mirage were colored by "thrill-seeking characters." As more and more people search for bits of the past to glamorize, this depiction has stuck. The rules have certainly changed. Changing times, money, and big-business concerns have rewoven the basic fabric of hot rodding over the years.

Today, the cost to become involved has much to do with the manner in which people involve themselves in hot rodding. Much like everything else in the world today, our little niche has grown into a huge industry made up of many segments and replacing that carefree automotive statement that was relatively unrestricted and ungoverned. I see it every day in our own offices and through the cars and trucks our people drive, both the real ones as well as the limited-edition desktop models.

Our offices have always been filled with *characters*; Pete had the uncanny knack of attracting them. One grown man has satisfied his automotive passion with the past by fully decorating his office with die-cast collectible cars ranging from tie-tack size to those you can pedal. These are interspersed with creatively built model cars in all sorts of situations, some housed in dioramas, another on a dragstrip launch pad doing a twisted wheelie. In Gray Baskerville's office, home of the world's oldest teenager, hangs everything from a custom-decorated 1932 Ford grille shell to posters of old Bakersfield drag races. He, too, has an odd assortment of hot rod "toy" cars, some made of wood, some broken, and one made into a pen desk set. There's enough Bonneville paraphernalia in his office to qualify for the beginnings of his own, personal museum. He drives a genuine hot rod to work, too.

There is certainly an affection for collecting tokens of the past, not only in the automotive field but in many areas of special interest. The publication you are holding in your hands will no doubt be considered a collectible, as its basic contents are historical elements. The preservation of historic materials has enabled the book's publication. It will be printed only once in our lifetime, and as a one-time anniversary tribute, will one day command collector-like value.

We can duplicate the parts and improve upon them, we can period-dress and hold 1950s-style parties and drive-ins, but we cannot bring back those times. We must move on. That was the founding principal of *Hot Rod*. Petersen himself said it in his very first editorial, "... *readers will find a chance to air their views, ask questions (and get answers), read about racing and timing meets and automobile shows, see the latest in engine and body designs, enjoy entertaining fiction and see engine parts displayed with what we call 'the feminine touch.'"* It is all there; we may have done it differently down through the years, but the mantle is

there. Even though it was later cloned by many, in the beginning, *Hot Rod* was the only magazine that brought insider insights to an information-starved nation. *Hot Rod* never just reported. From the beginning, *Hot Rod* has been intimately involved at all levels of rodding, from promoting early hot rod shows and introducing new car shows to providing the initial funding for the formation of the National Hot Rod Association (NHRA) under the untiring efforts of now-Chairman Wally Parks, our first full-time editor.

Each decade saw many innovations, from new types of events to an ever-widening array of distinctive cars and trucks. Much was created by the *Hot Rod* staff themselves, with the help and guidance of many other visionaries. At other times, the magazine played more of a developmental role in cultivating emerging trends. Insight, vision, and involvement are the primary ingredients of *Hot Rod* magazine. But the past is the past, today is now, and tomorrow is our challenge. We have always considered it our responsibility to build for tomorrow by, first, promoting the hobby of hot rodding and, second, by promoting all the various elements that go into the more vertical areas of interest that make up our entire marketplace.

We enjoy the milestones that have made *Hot Rod* magazine the world's leading automotive authority, and we do not take them lightly. This is why over the recent years, we have developed (or helped to develop) new, exciting activities like bringing back street-style (on the track, of course), heads-up racing. We remember that's where it all started. Now our National Muscle Car Association (both events *and* membership 1-800-248-7365) is growing like a weed. The *Hot Rod* TV show, aired

weekly on TNN, has exposed us to a TV generation who know little about the fun to be had while attending our events. They get to see firsthand the *Hot Rod* Power Festivals. They also witness the live building of various-style project cars, from streetable Mustangs to pavement-pounding Pro Street Camaros. *Hot Rod* has also joined with the Universal Technical Institute to offer special vocational courses to help the youth of today learn about repairing the ever-more-sophisticated systems in today's cars and trucks. We are also developing a scholarship awards program as one of a variety of new ways to reach the youth of today. We are even looking at ways to aid you in your drives to our events, and insuring your hot rod. The day is now upon us when *Hot Rod* will help finance the purchase and buildup of your first or next automotive project.

The youth of yesterday—you can find pictures of them and their cars throughout the following pages—are the leaders of the industry today. Their innovations and dedication are what made the difference for them and many others. Some very cool rides are the handiwork of these guys. We are particularly grateful to MBI Publishing Company, the specialists in automotive book publishing, for undertaking this effort, and to Tony Thacker for his undying dedication and willingness to search our archives for the material you find assembled within this publication. It is a fun perspective that highlights the decades with insightful anecdotes and some of the unique cars and events during the span of our 50 years of involvement. We hope you enjoy the trip.

—*John Dianna*
President
Automotive Performance Group

INTRODUCTION

In the beginning, there was enthusiasm and a lot of alkali dust kicked up by "gow jobs" flashing across the dry lake beds of Southern California. But there was no *Hot Rod* magazine. That came later.

Mankind's attraction to the automobile has created a society almost totally dependent on the motor vehicle for personal use, for livelihood, and for sport and personal satisfaction. With the motor vehicle's advantages, it has brought such problems as highway crowding, pollution and accidents. But if man was smart enough to create the vehicle in the first place, overcoming the present problems seems a comparatively small technological challenge.

The person who openly doesn't like motorized rolling stock has no idea what vehicles mean to people who appreciate cars. Some of the ultimate car-appreciating people are hot rodders, no matter what kind of cars they own, or what kind of racing they enjoy. There is no set definition of a hot rodder, other than a person who modifies his or her car for increased performance or improved appearance. Henry Ford, Gottlieb Daimler, and Barney Oldfield all fit the description as easily as Ronnie Sox, Don Garlits, or Richard Petty. They all share(d) the desire to individually improve a car and its engine.

The terms "hot rod," "hot rodding" and "hot rodders" are relatively new to the automotive world only because they were coined late in the progress of the automobile. The "hot rod" tag came to flower initially in California apparently a contraction of the term "hot roadster" from the early

Robert E. Petersen, the man behind *Hot Rod* and Petersen Publishing Company.

1940s. However, hot rodding on a noticeable level began just after the turn of the century, as soon as there were cars. Racers gathered on board tracks, highways, beach fronts and paved ovals any time there seemed to be a good reason. With the low-cost, simple-to-work-on, and easy-to-obtain Ford Model T came hundreds of small companies building accessories for it. By 1920, anyone who wanted to put a little more suds in his car could order the necessary pieces from a mail order catalog. Naturally, this spawned an unholy explosion of racing, the bulk of it spur-of-the-moment contests held whenever and wherever it seemed fitting. But street racing was no less dangerous then than now.

Citizens didn't care for it, and as time and the danger went on, there were many attempts at finding legitimate racing areas. Some succeeded; many failed. The fact remains that any time a person is given the opportunity to improve his machine, a competitive spirit that predates a Cro-Magnon bully taking on the village heavyweight at the local cavern will emerge. More cars and more people dictated more control.

Hot rodding's pioneers came from all types of backgrounds, and rich and poor shared a common interest—making a car work better, faster and longer. Acknowledged as the sire of hot rodding is the late Ed Winfield. Winfield was born just after the turn of the century, and his love for automobiles was evident long before he was old enough to shave. He grew up in the outskirts of Los Angeles, and his first rod was based on Model T Ford components. That was nearly 80 years ago. Winfield was one of the first to realize that performance equipment was quite often unavailable for his particular application, and some of what was available was often marginal in value and/or a long time in arriving once it had been ordered. The simple answer was to make what one needed. This step gave birth to the speed and specialty equipment industry, that today is a major part of American economics.

Yesterday's hot rodder didn't often think of that, nor would he have cared. His concern was his own machine. Early hot rodders were mostly "amateurs" in that they practiced their art without promise of monetary return. Professionalism did exist, with names like Deusenberg, Chevrolet,

An early hot rod show at the Los Angeles City Armory, 1949.

Miller, and Ford representing factory involvement in all-out racing. Factory participation in racing is nothing new. From the earliest days of auto racing contests, car makers were right in the thick of it, and on a much grander scale than in recent years. In the book *Ford: The Dust And The Glory, A Racing History*, author Leo Levine traces Ford racing involvement from 1901, with Henry himself doing a lot of the arranging and some of the driving. Specially built cars were the order of the day; few rules existed, and they were subject to quick change. Auto companies considered racing necessary to sell cars, and the faster they could make cars run, the better everyone liked it. Aftermarket equipment companies benefited from all this, as they do now, and hero drivers soon realized the worth of their endorsement on products.

Not the least concerned with what was happening elsewhere, the Southern California hot rodding contingent blossomed and did things with cars that theoretically couldn't be done. The communication gap between those eastern professionals and the western amateurs proved over and over that ignorance really can be bliss. Legions of sun-tanned enthusiasts worked over their four-cylinder T engines, or any engine they happened to have. And as soon as they had something in running condition, they took it out for a bit of racing. Racing meant anywhere, anytime, and against anything. There was no such thing as formal drag racing, a type of contest not even named until the 1930s.

California's topography includes dry lakes, landmarks almost exclusive to the western part of the country and ideal for running a car flat out. Dry lakes meets became monthly events, and sometimes were held more often, providing an early-day hot rodder cared to drive the distance. Unlike today's orderly, safety-oriented, and properly sanctioned dry lakes speed trials where only one car goes at a time, early dry lakes activities were nearly riotous in nature. If the lake being used was wide enough for 20 cars, then 20 cars might race at one time. Pity the poor guy who didn't have enough horsepower to be at, or keep up with, the lead. Dry lakes are notoriously dusty, and trailing *any* car on a lake bed accounts for zero visibility. Those days were filled with sensational newspaper accounts of mass slaughter on those barren grounds, where the so-called demons of death and destruction gathered to wage war against each other. The outlaw stigma attached itself to hot rodders, and present-day chopper motorcycle riders can't begin to know what harassment and low public opinion is like, compared to the wrath and scorn aimed at hot rodders of four decades ago.

The Francisco Family Reunion featured the hot rod "Mexican Jaguar." A fatigued technical editor, "Poppa Don" Francisco" supervises from the prone position in the lower right.

A ray of hope in turning the tide of public opinion was first seen in the formation of the Southern California Timing Association, (S.C.T.A.) which Art Tilton organized in 1937. Rules on racing conduct and safety helped clean up dry lakes racing, but since few journalists cared to visit the lakes at that time (or to this day for that matter), most of the orderly racing went unnoticed in the daily press. Street racing was, and still is, the greatest threat to the existence of hot rodders. Member clubs of S.C.T.A. set up volunteer patrols to discourage street racing by their members and other hot rodders. A hot rodder didn't have to be a member of S.C.T.A. to get caught racing on the street and make a bad impression with the local citizenry.

The threat of involvement in World War II brought the Army Air Corps to the lake beds of California, and it took over the most famous of them all: Muroc. It is now Edwards Air Force Base, and within a couple of years of the Army's setting up camp on Muroc, many former lakes racers found themselves back at Muroc, working not on hot rods but on airplanes. World War II almost put a halt to hot rodding, yet the hot rodders themselves learned much from the military, and they contributed much. The Air Corps' famed Henry Arnold (Hap) gave high endorsement to the men of the hot rod movement during the war when he stated that, if given a choice, he'd take hot rodders to fly his planes.

When World War II ended, hot rodders returned home with newfound mechanical talents and maturity. Because they had gone off to war, these ex-servicemen were treated respectfully, and their hot rodding antics were observed with less disdain. This is a heck of a way to gain acceptance, but history is filled with oddities.

Southern California hot rodders soon found new devotees to this sport. The shipping-out points at West Coast ports had brought many an eastern lad to California during the war, and thousands of them remembered the warm winter weather, clear skies (that was a long time ago), open spaces, and millions of orange trees where the fruit was free for the picking. Thus began the overpopulation of California, and in numbers there is strength.

Ironically, the scrap metal drives of the war had cleaned the country of old cars, and in the years directly following the war, it didn't matter what kind of car you bought, it cost too much. Those who had cars used their mechanical skills acquired in the military to maintain and improve them, and customizing became an art form. George and Sam Barris became the heroes of the customizing clan, and George Cerny, whose son is now active in the custom paint scene, ran a well-stocked customizing shop within earshot of the Barris emporium. Customizers were a breed apart from traditional hot rodders, such as Vic Edelbrock, Sr., and drive-in restaurants would generally be the stand-off points for each group. One side of the parking area would be filled with fenderless coupes and roadsters, the other packed with Carson-topped, fender-skirted Mercs and 1940 Fords, and "the twain never met."

Racing areas became harder to find after the war, thanks to the almost totally unchecked population explosion in southern California. Dry lakes racers returned to El Mirage, but newfound speeds and equipment made for precarious racing on the relatively short lake bed. S.C.T.A. founder Art Tilton didn't come home after the war, but the association was strong, and its one paid employee at the time was a young hot rodder and talented organizer by the name of Wally Parks. He and his fellow S.C.T.A. members recognized the threat to racing safety at El Mirage, so for a

This middle eliminator, 1961, featured Lew Grubtill from Omaha, Nebraska, driving his 1938 Fiat with a 301-cubic inch 1948 Mercury and Paul Powell of Louisville, Nebraska, powered to victory by a 296-cubic inch 1948 Mercury.

place to go high-speed running, they looked toward the Bonneville Salt Flats.

However, the salt flats had been used for years under sanction of the American Automobile Association (AAA), and the Triple A's opinion of rodders using it was akin to having a mother-in-law move in for an extended vacation. They didn't want us on the salt. The AAA didn't own the salt, but many years of sanctioning speed trials there had given it a powerful lobby voice with the Salt Lake City officials who controlled its use. Many visits to Salt Lake City by Wally Parks, Bob Petersen and Lee Ryan and other S.C.T.A. representatives led to discovery of an ally on the city staff

in the form of Gus Bachman. He had heard of the hot rod movement in California, and believed it could be good for Utah. Bachman felt the presence of a large group of racing enthusiasts could be an economic help to the normally deserted area around Wendover.

It took a concerted effort by Gus and the S.C.T.A. representatives to even get the hot rodders' case heard, but in the late months of 1948, permission was granted to stage the first Bonneville Speed Week. Ironically, once the meet became a date on the calendar, resistance from some S.C.T.A. members cropped up. In order to run on the salt, the Southern California Timing Association had

to purchase insurance for the meet, which it did, and it had to pay Otto Crocker for his timing equipment. The S.C.T.A. treasury wasn't empty. In fact, there were times during its formative years when there were over 1,000 dues-paying members. But those members who either couldn't get away long enough or afford the trip, objected to withdrawing several hundred dollars from the kitty to pay for the enjoyment of a select few. Cries of woe, cheating, and outright stealing eventually were silenced, and the money was taken from the treasury.

Coinciding with the S.C.T.A.'s search for a new playground and its rise in hot rodding popularity, was the entrance to this

Hot Rod has been involved with drag racing from the very beginning. Here, Petersen looks over an early 1960s short-wheelbase top gas dragster.

automotive arena by a young man named Bob Petersen. Petersen's father was a mechanic, and Bob was interested in cars and hot rodding. Here is his hot rodding background, in his words: "I built cars and played around with them. Nothing too spectacular. Bob Lindsay (his friend and cofounder of *Hot Rod* magazine) and I had done a lot of things around hot rods. Lindsay's father had a magazine, and between us—with his father's help—we started on the first issue of *Hot Rod*. We'd seen what was happening and thought it would be a good idea for a magazine."

Execution of the first issue of *Hot Rod* began in 1947, and, while Petersen and Lindsay were getting started, Pete lost his publicity job with MGM. He then joined the Hollywood Publicity Associates. Pete and his partners in this company got a job promoting Earl Muntz (Mad Man), a legendary figure from Los Angeles' early days of loud-voiced, fender-banging, used car salesmanship, and the man who later on established the Muntz car stereo company. The Hollywood Associates were working on a plan to develop Southern California's first real drag strip by first putting on a car show, then using the proceeds from that to build the Earl Muntz drag strip. Difficulties arose, and there never was a Muntz drag strip. But the car show idea remained, and Petersen and the Hollywood Publicity Associates and the S.C.T.A. combined to stage a car show at the Armory in Exposition Park in 1948. The show was a terrific success, both in financial return and enlightening the public about hot rodders. Once the public got a look at the quality and engineering of customs and rods, and was afforded a look at the people who built and drove them, hot rodders became a more tolerated part of society. S.C.T.A. derived publicity and revenue from the hot rod show. The publicity group churned gobs of promotion that it couldn't have obtained on its own. With Petersen doing the magazine and still remaining a part of the Hollywood Publicity Associates, some of his partners thought he should relinquish one or the other.

"I told them I'd put the magazine into the deal, but that I wanted to be the only one representing it, since Lindsay and I started it. But they said that sounded like a lousy deal, so the three of them said they'd take the show instead if I'd relinquish my quarter interest." Petersen related this turn of events to us recently, and while it turned out much better for him, he couldn't forecast that at the time. Petersen and Lindsay had invested $200 each in the company, and the first print order was for 10,000 magazines. "We used to take them to the races and sell them in the stands at the lakes when we weren't out shooting pictures. At night we'd hit all the drive-ins around L.A., and use the money to go inside and eat," Petersen explained. "Our printing was done by a little outfit down in L.A., and one of the printers who worked there loved to play the horses, but he usually lost. When he got deep in debt, he'd call me to ask for some money. In return for my cash, he'd print up a few hundred extra copies and write them off as 'waste.' We kept it rather quiet, naturally, but everyone was so broke in those days, especially me, that we'd do most anything to save on expenses." Petersen Publishing in 1948 was not a major economic threat to this country's publishing houses. "We didn't have carpeted offices or sweet-smelling secretaries, and we most certainly weren't on the invitation list for press parties."

Bob Petersen remembers *Hot Rod's* initial venture to Indianapolis for the "500," a facility where we are now welcomed and accepted. "We were looked upon as outlaws. The three-A hated us and thought we were a bunch of real bad guys. We had a Wayne GMC-engined car called the *Hot Rod* Magazine Special entered in the race, and Don Francisco and Wally Parks were part of the crew. The race officials kept trying to wipe the name off the car. They didn't want any car in *their* race with a name like '*Hot Rod*' on it. We had nothing but trouble with them. Later on, we had a car with our name on it that Alex Xydias and Dean Batchelor took to Daytona to run on the beach. France's (Bill France) NASCAR crew made us wipe out the name on the side of the car facing the spectators. Anyway, the car crashed and you know what side of it they got pictures of then."

A few years after that first issue, Bob Lindsay left Petersen. During that time he was with Petersen, *Motor Trend* had been started, and in October 1949, Wally Parks became the first official editor of *Hot Rod*. The name and the term *Hot Rod* was starting to mean something worthwhile, but a lot of Pete's associates maintained he ought to get rid of the name for the sake of respectability. But he decided it was better to face up to the challenge and live with the name that had become a nationally known phrase. He knew something had to be done to establish hot rodding as a major force and sport.

When the S.C.T.A. went to Bonneville, the racers who couldn't go still wanted to do some racing, and this gave birth to drag racing on a semi-organized level. There was nothing new about racing from a standing start, because hot rodders had been doing that on the street for years. There have been many claims as to where the first "official" (meaning *not* on the street) drag race was held, and rather than instigate further argument, we'll just say that the earliest known drags were held at Goleta airport near Santa Barbara, which is north of Los Angeles, and at the old blimp hangar area in Tustin, California on what is now John Wayne International Airport. One thing is for sure: There were a lot more attempts at getting a drag racing site than there were drag strips in the pre-1950 days. Civic leaders were hardly cordial to the pleas of hot rodders, who obviously were irresponsible no-goods bent on destroying themselves and everyone

13

around them. Finally, in the summer of 1950, C. J. Hart and Frank Stillwell conducted the first legal drag race at the site of the current John Wayne airport. There wasn't any prize money involved, and only blatantly obvious unsafe cars were turned away. Nobody realized it at the time, but this was the event that made hot rodding a project that could be enjoyed all over the world, not just in California or on the dry lakes or over the salt of Bonneville.

Robert E. Petersen remembers what turned the tide for hot rodding: "The two big things that got it off the ground were Bonneville and the National Hot Rod Association. Wally (Parks) started it in 1951, when he was Editor of *Hot Rod* and he got all the guys together, like Bud Coons and (Eric) Rickman, who later went on the Safety Safaris for NHRA in 1954 and 1955. That was the biggest thing for *Hot Rod* and hot rodding. They started organizing racing, and got a lot more people interested in us and the sport. We had to sell ourselves to various civic groups. We had big battles here in Los Angeles with the National Safety Council and the P.T.A. I remember there was a nice little old lady in the P.T.A. who liked me—she thought I was a sweet kid—and that really helped. There were a lot of good guys who helped us back then, and are still around, like Wally, Ak Miller, Rick (Eric Rickman), Bud Coons and Lee Ryan. Their good behavior, appearance and conduct really surprised most non-hot rod types, who had preconceived notions about what to expect. These guys really helped us, and I'm glad to see they've all done well for themselves since then."

Word travels fast when it involves something popular, like hot rodding. After

From its inception, *Hot Rod* has been dedicated to the do-it-yourself hobbyist.

the early issues of the magazine were sold at race tracks, they found their way all over the country, and pretty soon there were letters coming from around the United States, wanting to know how to get more copies. "We didn't have much of a circulation system established. We were mailing magazines all over the nation," Pete remembers. "Some went to speed shops, and a lot went to big newsstands in large cities. Once we got the magazine selling in a lot of somewhat unusual—for us—places, we took it down to a big stand in Hollywood and left about 50 copies. The owner said he'd try and sell some, but he didn't act too optimistic. About a day later he called back and said they were all gone and told us to bring some more. Pretty soon we were taking them to a lot of big stands around town, and if they didn't think they could sell 'em, we'd tell them to call that first newsstand and find out how well they sold."

Half a century and 600 issues later, our heads our still swimming with 50-years-worth of great magazine stories and photos: lakes cars, belly tankers, wide whites, roadsters, scallops, speed records, custom Mercs, flagmen, gassers, innovative engines, early floppers, swimsuit gals, vans, murals, music, jet cars, flame jobs, stockers, muscle cars, movies, Pro Streeters, resto rods, rusto rods, and all those *Hot Rod* project cars. It's been a wild ride, hasn't it?

As we look back through all of these images, we realize that *Hot Rod* magazine isn't just about cars, it's also about people. But of all the people who have contributed to the success of hot rodding and *Hot Rod* magazine over the years, the most important ones hardly ever get their names or their faces in the magazine: the readers. It's *Hot Rod*'s readers who really set the trends, provide the news, and constantly move hot rodding in new directions. Without you, this whole 50-year ride would've ended with the first issue. Our hope is that you have been as inspired, educated, motivated, excited, informed, and entertained by *Hot Rod* magazine as we have been by you. We've got another 50-years-worth of magazine to fill, so keep it coming. Thanks for reading.

—*Tony Thacker*

THE FIFTIES

JUNE 1959
In 1959, the team of Fred Larsen and Don Cummins, synonymous with lakes racing, fielded this sano '29 Model A roadster pickup, powered by a Hilborn-injected 1954 Chrysler. Fred turned 193 miles per hour on straight alky at the dry lakes and also won the Best Appearing Car trophy at the Russetta Timing Association meet. Steering was from a 1934 Ford and the transmission was a rare 1939 Lincoln, ideal for a center-steering car because of its right-hand side cover and floor shift lever.

Chapter 1

Driveway Mechanics to Crosswalk Cruisers

Even though *Hot Rod* had been in existence for two years and had 24 issues of *The Automotive 'HOW-TO-DO-IT'* magazine under its belt, *Hot Rod* was still a regional publication. However, two major events would totally transform this 36-page collection of track roadster, dry lake, and reliability run coverage, mixed with Stromberg carb mods and Rex Burnett cutaways, into a 124-page package filled with the latest Super Stock tests, national drag racing coverage, 23 pages of "roto"-section car features, 400-plus-mile per hour tires, go-karts, engine overviews, mags, Mr. Eliminators, and a guy called Ed Byrnes (Kookie). *Hot Rod* became everybody's automotive magazine because of two Ds: the drags and Detroit.

Hot Rod began covering drag racing on a regular basis when C. J. Hart (Pappy) began staging weekly drags at the Orange County Airport in April 1950. The impact was twofold. First, hot rodders no longer needed to make the trek to a dry lake or salt flat to race—they could do it in their backyard. Second was a response to a letter sent to *Hot Rod* by reader Bob Cameron, from Chicago, Illinois. Cameron's letter, which appeared in the March 1951 issue, posed the question, "Why not form a nationwide hot rod association that covers all aspects of hot rodding?" By May 1951, the National Hot Rod Association, under the leadership of editor Wally Parks, was a reality.

The first U.S. Nationals was held in Great Bend, Kansas, in 1955, and this ultimately led to Detroit's involvement. Two years prior, a hot rodding engineer, Zora Arkus Duntov, wrote his bosses at Chevrolet a memo titled, "Thoughts Pertaining to Youth, Hot Rodders, and Chevrolet." Duntov was able to capsulize just what this car craze was all about and management's decision to embrace Duntov's thoughts transformed Chevrolet, and then the rest of Detroit, from a Midwest mentality to a youth-market orientation.

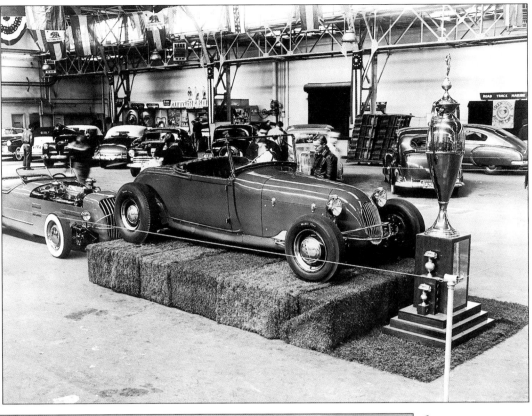

MARCH 1950

Although there was an automotive show held in 1949, the first National Roadster Show was held in Oakland in 1950. With exactly 100 cars in the show, 26,624 visitors came to see Bill Niekamp of Compton, California, win the big one for a track roadster that *Hot Rod* described as, "Neither flashy, spectacular or even tested for speed." However, author Griff Borgeson went on to say, "What is remarkable about the car, and the feature that enabled it to take seven other major awards, is the perfect purity of its layout and workmanship." Bill did eventually run 142.40 miles per hour at El Mirage in 1952. The Niekamp roadster is currently owned and was restored by Jim Jacobs (Jake).

MAY 1950

The cover of the May 1950 issue, photographed by Tom Medley, depicted two young hot rodders bent intently over the rear-mounted, 156-cubic inch V-8-60-powered 1927 T roadster. The two young men were Ray Brown, of Ray Brown Automotive, on the left, and Alex Xydias of the SO-CAL Speed Shop on the right. The roadster ran 134.73 miles per hour at the June 1949 SCTA meet, and both men went on to become hugely successful and prominent in the hot rod industry.

In the August 1950 issue, Don Francisco reported on the June 10 and 11 SCTA Speedfest held at El Mirage where, "Top speeds continued their upward sweep." In this typical dry lakes scene, two belly tanks are instantly recognizable. On the left, number 123C is the "C" class lakester driven by Jim Johnston. Constructed for hospitalized George Castera by Bill Burke, the car took its class record with a two-way average of 157.235. The tank had a frame constructed of strut tubing, with a 276-inch Merc engine. To its right is the *Evans Special*. Using an early V-8, with Bob Ward behind the wheel it ran 150.25 miles per hour but it also held the SCTA Lakester one-way top speed of 172 miles per hour, using a big-bore Mercury engine.

SEPTEMBER 1950

Hot rods, in the early days, tended to evolve as young enthusiasts experimented and developed their own ways of going faster. One infamous young tinkerer was Don Waite, and these two photographs show the evolutionary process of his 1927 T roadster. In 1947, Don, of Temple City, California, was using the roadster to deliver eggs from his father's ranch. Numbered 524B and with Don looking tall in the saddle, his first racing effort had a Cragar four-barrel engine mounted in the rear, hence his strange, forward-mounted position. At the end of the 1948 season, the car was converted to V-8 power and, as the car came down, the speeds went up. By 1950, it was a sleek, stylish trackster that ran 160.71 miles per hour. Incidentally, the motor was mounted on a quick-release frame that could be wheeled out from under the car.

MAY 1951

In the first issue to feature a color photograph on the cover, incidentally of Jack Morgan's channeled 1934 roadster, the Hot Rod of The Month was Art Gerrick's Rajo four-banger–powered track T. Built in that timeless track roadster style, the car is as cool today as it was 50 years ago.

APRIL 1951

Though never actually featured within the pages of *Hot Rod* magazine, this rather rudimentary roadster with its odd looking front and rear sub frames, was the means by which *Hot Rod* captured those great photographs at Bonneville in 1952. The car, a 1927 track roadster that belonged to Manuel Ayulo, was converted to the HRM "camera car" early in 1951. Incidentally, Manuel and Jack McGrath teamed up to compete in the 1951 running of the Indy 500.

AUGUST 1951
Another regular series that ran in the 1950s was "Touring The Hot Rod Shops," and although photographed in August 1951, *Hot Rod*'s visit to Ray Brown Automotive was never published. Here then, for the first time ever, is an unpublished shot of Ray's shop. The car to the left was Ray's own "A" Class roadster, which placed first in the May 1951 Russetta meet, with a speed of 124.309 miles per hour. In the middle was Earl Evans Merc-powered belly tank, which set a "C" class record of 181.080 miles per hour at the July SCTA meet.

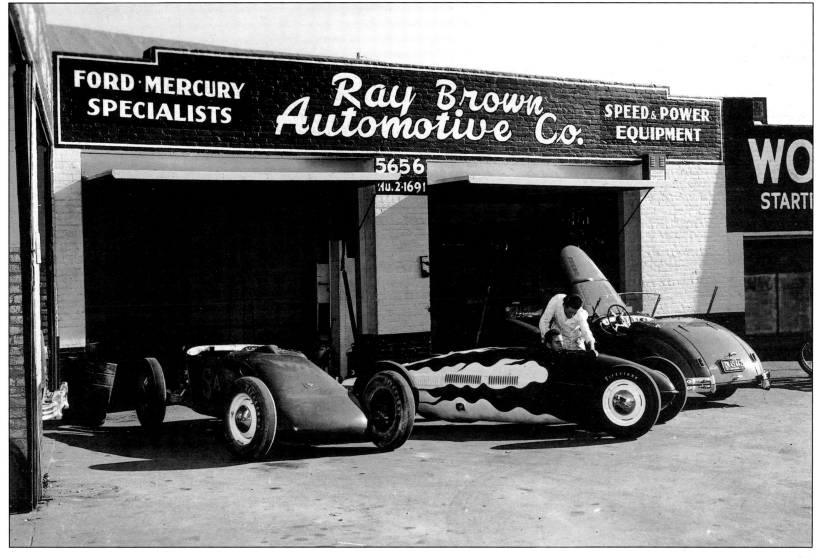

NOVEMBER 1951

Of all the world's auto racing venues, nothing compares to the Bonneville Salt Flats. Possibly one of the most inhospitable spots on the planet, Bonneville remains a mecca for true hot rodders. Each year they make the pilgrimage from all over the world to, more often than not, stand ankle-deep in wet salt and watch their creations disappear over the curvature of the earth. These two shots from the 1951 meet graphically depict both the vastness of the Flats and the closeness of the participants. The Circle of Champions included many *Hot Rod* regulars, including Alex Xydias' SO-CAL belly tank, and in the center, the September 1951 cover car, Bill Kenz's twin-engined "D" Class record-holding streamliner, which ran 210 miles per hour in 1950.

SEPTEMBER 1951
For many hot rodders, building small-scale versions of their cars has always been a fun and enjoyable part of the hobby—it's another type of bench racing. Here, Al Jimenez of San Juan Capistrano, California, using a Rex Burnett cutaway published in *Hot Rod* for reference, adds a final dab of paint to his finely detailed, flathead-powered track roadster. Where is it now?

'52

MAY 1952

The formative years of hot rodding are so interesting to look back on because of the experimentation. Unsophisticated hot rodders attempting to break new ground worked largely by trial and error in their pursuit of speed secrets. For example, Bob Garrett's modified roadster *Ant Eater* had its Speedomotive-equipped V-8-60, which was fitted with a front-driven blower, mounted just ahead of the rear end. Driver Hal Osborne sat ahead of the cowl and behind part of a chopped-off belly tank. The car, perhaps one of the first to have a flip-up body, held the SCTA "D" roadster record, as well as the Russetta "B" roadster record. What's really cool, though, is the method by which the numbers were applied.

APRIL 1952

The cover blurb of the April '52 issue said, "We Channeled and Chopped Our Car at Home." Inside, *Hot Rod* gave a good account with how-to illustrations, of how Glenn and Vivian Johnson remodeled their 1937 Ford coupe. Amazingly enough, the car remained in constant use while Glenn hacked it about. Sadly, as the project neared completion after two years of work, a spark from a smoldering rag caught the gas tank on fire and the car was gutted. Undeterred, Glenn found it much easier the "second time around."

JULY 1952

Early hot rods were not always the most reliable means of transport, and in 1948 the Pasadena Roadster Club initiated an event called the Reliability Run. This event offered car owners and their families the opportunity to participate in a sporting event in which a point system based on strict observance of the California State Vehicle Code was used to determine the winners. The concept grew quickly, due to exposure in *Hot Rod* magazine. The July '52 *Hot Rod* covered a reliability run in Ohio, organized by the Miami Valley Chapter of the NHRA. Here, at the starting line, is Corrie Holloway with his A-V-8 roadster, along with the trophies that would be awarded to the winners.

OCTOBER 1952

In its ongoing effort to legitimize the sport, *Hot Rod* magazine initiated a Public Service Award. In 1952, it was presented to the Road Angels, a member club of the Columbia Timing Association, located in Oregon. Here, Oregon Governor Douglas McKay, who spent 32 years in the automotive business and was very sympathetic toward the hot rod movement, checks out a club member's 1927 T with a two-port Riley. The Road Angels made McKay an honorary member.

JANUARY 1953
A major attraction at the 1952 Motorama was Roy Dunn's Valley Custom-built '50 Ford Tudor. Shown here during construction, the body was shortened 5 inches; the wheel wells were radiused; it was nosed, decked and shaved; and it featured a very tidy interior.

JANUARY 1953

Featured on the cover of the February 1952 edition, Earl Bruce's 1940 Ford coupe was the product of 10 years of constant reconstruction. Powered by an Eddie Meyer-prepared Mercury flathead, the chopped coupe was distinctive because of its filled rear quarter windows, rounded door corners, shaved handles and bright red paint. In 1953, *Hot Rod* revisited the car, at that time in the hands of Valley Custom, where it was getting a new lacquer paint job. Bruce still owns this car, which is now blue.

MAY 1953
Another popular series was "Prove it on the Dyno," and the May 1953 *Hot Rod* checked out the Meyer-Drake 270-inch Offy. The engine was, of course, one of the winningest in motorsports history.

JUNE 1953
Frank Rose entered this beautiful fendered track-style 1927 T roadster in the 1953 Grand National Roadster Show, no doubt in hope of winning the America's Most Beautiful Roadster Award. Unfortunately, he didn't win, and the 9-foot trophy went to Dick Williams' light blue '27. Undeterred, Frank returned the following year with red scallops and white pinstriping by Tommy the Greek over the blue base and took home the big one. The car, which featured the metal shaping of Jack Hagemann, still exists.

DECEMBER 1953
Despite all the nights spent by hot rodders in the drive-ins across the nation, very few photographs remain depicting those events and locations. Fewer still remain of the Carousel drive-in in Los Angeles, where *Hot Rod* photographed Jack McDermott's 1929 on 1932 rails for the cover of the December '53 issue. Jack's roadster was powered by a 268-inch 1946 Merc with a 1934 transmission. It was painted by Barris Kustom and fitted with a Gaylord interior, and employed reworked 1937 Buick spare tire covers for its unusual fenders.

FEBRUARY 1954
Hot Rod, Promised the most fantastic
coupe complete with construction details.

DO A BETTER VALVE JOB By Don Francisco

HOT ROD

The Automotive "HOW-TO-DO-IT" Magazine

FORD FORSAKES THE FLATHEADS!

New OHV Engine Family

FEBRUARY 1954 25c

THE MOST FANTASTIC COUPE!

CONSTRUCTION DETAILS—163 MPH RECORD HOLDER

JUNE 1954

Two distinctly different styles here. On the left, Jim St. Claire's "Road Race Rod" cover car, which won a first, a second, and two third places in Southern California sports car events. Jim handled most of the engine and chassis work on this 276-inch Merc-motored 1934 coupe himself. Alongside Jim is his buddy Orin Brown from El Segundo, California, with his equally smooth, fully fendered "deuce."

JUNE 1954

Pomona is a name synonymous with drag racing. Now the permanent home of the NHRA Winternationals, Pomona was home to its first drag race back in 1951 at the old Fontana Airport. Eventually the Pomona Choppers convinced the city of Pomona that the club could prove itself worthy of community respect. Working under the title of the Pomona Valley Timing Association (PVTA), the group enjoyed the loan of city funds to develop their strip. The PVTA also boasted two club-owned cars, one a 1934 coupe and the other a sleek dragster. Most of the work and driving chores were handled by Dawson Hadley, while Ed Vogel hammered out the svelte body, using parts from aluminum aircraft belly tanks. The car is shown here in unpainted form on one of its first outings and also in final form when the front brakes had been removed and the body reshaped. The car was powered by a fuel-injected Chrysler Hemi.

JULY 1954

While few dealers specialize in used hot rods and customs, Custom City in Santa Monica, California, billed itself as the "World's Largest Custom and Hot Rod Lot." Operated by Marvin Gelberg and Park Dana, Custom City sold everything, including this little belly tank-bodied Formula III racer in street trim and powered by a four-cylinder, air-cooled, Indian motorcycle engine. The channeled 1932 coupe was purchased in rough condition and when these pictures were taken, was part way through refurbishment by Custom City staff.

AUGUST 1954

As drag racing evolved from illegal street racing to an organized, international sport, the NHRA constantly upgraded its regulations to improve the sport's safety. In the August 1954 issue, *Hot Rod* published the NHRA rules. This rather busy, but basically sound, 1934 coupe was used to illustrate the Altered Coupe/Sedan category.

32

AUGUST 1954
Among the Reliability Runs and other endurance-type events, one of the best known was the Mobil Gas Economy Run. Automobiles to compete in the Run were entered, with few exceptions, by automobile dealers and dealer associations, apparent in this unpublished photograph of cars getting ready to leave. In the 1954 running of the marathon from Los Angeles to Sun Valley, J. C. Agajanian was the official starter and Clay Smith was one of the drivers. In the High Price Automatic Drive class, the Chrysler Custom Imperial in the foreground averaged 16.4463 miles per gallon, while the best economy went to a Studebaker Champion Custom, which averaged an almost-double 29.5806 miles per gallon.

'55

JANUARY 1955

Jack Webb's *Dragnet* was one of the most popular TV detective thrillers of all time and was certainly highly rated in the mid-1950s when Bob D'Olivo photographed him for the cover of the January 1955 issue. While Webb is shown with Tom Pollard and his bright red highboy roadster, the car, which has a Barris Kustom crest both on the cowl and in the windshield, was not actually featured in the show. It wasn't even featured in that issue of *Hot Rod*. Tom's 1929 on Deuce rails was eventually painted lime green and flamed by Barris before being striped by Von Dutch.

FEBRUARY 1955

The cover of the February 1955 issue was a scene from Bonneville—pure *Hot Rod*. Inside, however, two very different stories peaked the interest of serious aficionados. The first, by Racer Brown, was titled "Viva Ensalada" and covered the 1954 and fifth running of the Carrera Panamericana Mexico. As you can see, spectators came out in the thousands to see, among others, Ak Miller in the *Hot Rod*-sponsored *El Caballo*. The Mexicans nicknamed the *Hot Rod* entry *La Ensalada,* which meant it was made up of all kinds of parts. Ak came fifth in the Large Sport Car class and seventh overall behind a fleet of Ferraris driven by Maglioli, Phil Hill and Luigi Chinetti.

FEBRUARY 1955
Another sports car/hot rod of great importance featured in the February 1955 issue was that of Frank Kurtis. The *500-X*, designed for sports car competition, was from Kurtis Kraft, the shop that was responsible that year for 9 out of the first 10 cars to finish the Indy 500. Here, Kurtis, the tall guy on the right, expounds on a recent 2,500-mile Firestone tire test to Ed Walsh, Alfred Momo, racing driver Stirling Moss and development engineer/driver Ken Miles. Less engine—a variety including Chevy, Chrysler Hemi and even an Offy were optional—and transmission, the *500-X* sold for around $6,000.

APRIL 1955
Occasionally, hot rodders took to the hills, and in the April 1955 issue *Hot Rod* visited the Strippers Club of Denver and the club's second annual Georgetown, Colorado, hill climb. Beginning in the middle of Georgetown, at an elevation of 8,500 feet, the race was staged over 2 1/8 miles, and was open to both open and closed cars. Even a few dragsters competed. However, Bob Graham in his deuce five-window, shown here getting the flag from trophy girl Gerry Straface, was never challenged for first position. Bob took the hill in 2 minutes, 3.16 seconds, and beat the next car by 11 seconds.

OCTOBER 1955

Hot Rod has always had room for a little humor, and in the October 1955 issue, Lester Nehamkin visited the recently opened Disneyland to experience the Richfield Oil Corporation's mile-long roadway. Powered by 7 1/2-horsepower Mustang motorcycle engines mounted under Glasspar fiberglass bodies, the cars had a flat-out speed of 10 miles per hour. They looked like a whole lotta fun, especially the police version, which had cop brakes and a cop motor and could hit 25 miles per hour to catch the speeding little tikes and their moms.

'56

FEBRUARY 1956
It would be called sacrilege now, but in 1956, *Hot Rod*'s Eric Rickman told readers, "Join The Fun—Build A Jalopy." Of course, the fad for jalopy racing early Ford coupes decimated the numbers, as the cars were basically stripped down to bare essentials. Perhaps, however, that just made those that remained all the more valuable.

APRIL 1956
They couldn't get away with it today, but in 1956 there were several all-girl car clubs. From Denver, Colorado, it was "The Stripperettes," from Houston Texas, it was "The Powder Puff Bandits," while another group out of Mill Valley, California, was called "The Skirts." They fielded an impressive array of automobiles.

AUGUST 1956
Roadsters took on many shapes in the try-it-and see formative 1950s, and some of the influences were European in origin. Harry Rootlieb's hybrid 1941, for example, looked like a European sports car but was, in fact, fabricated from various early Fords including a 1933 Tudor and a 1949 Merc. Under the patchwork hood, and behind the 1935 Ford truck grille resided a stock 1950 Olds V-8. Despite this mixed parentage, Rootlieb's roadster garnered many prizes at the Los Angeles' Motor Revue.

DECEMBER 1956
After years of exploiting hot rods, Hollywood turned around somewhat in the mid-1960s and began showing them in a better light.

OCTOBER 1956
When *Hot Rod* heralded "A New Car - A New Challenge," the magazine was, of course, talking about Ak Miller's *El Caballo II*. The original T-bodied car (shown in the background) was built for the Mexican Road Race, but when the race was canceled, it was decided to groom *Caballo* for the Italian Mille Miglia. This reader-backed car was based on a modified Speedway chassis given by Frank Kurtis. Power was provided by a Danny Eames/Chrysler Corp.-donated 1957 Chrysler with Hilborn injection, W&H two-coil ignition, Howard F-4 cam and Jahns pistons. The aluminum body was being built by Jack Sutton.

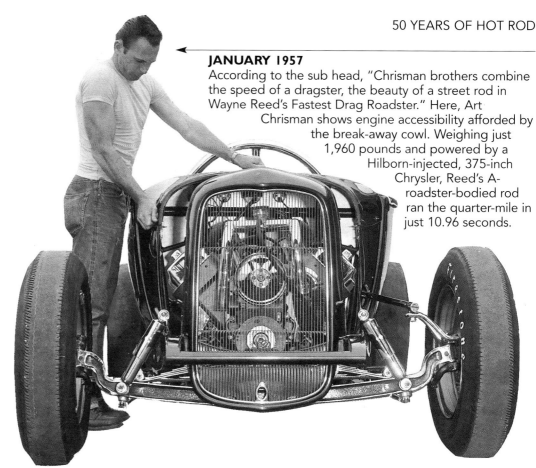

JANUARY 1957
According to the sub head, "Chrisman brothers combine the speed of a dragster, the beauty of a street rod in Wayne Reed's Fastest Drag Roadster." Here, Art Chrisman shows engine accessibility afforded by the break-away cowl. Weighing just 1,960 pounds and powered by a Hilborn-injected, 375-inch Chrysler, Reed's A-roadster-bodied rod ran the quarter-mile in just 10.96 seconds.

JUNE 1957
Obviously, aerodynamics were in their infancy in 1957 when contractor A. E. Burgess took this 1957 Chrysler-powered 1938 Plymouth to Daytona for speed trials. With a McCulloch blower and Bob Reuther behind the wheel, the coupe went 150.25 miles per hour and bumped the NASCAR Modified record 13 miles per hour.

AUGUST 1957
After winning the very first America's Most Beautiful Roadster Award at the 1950 Oakland Roadster Show, with a car that doubled as both a show and go rod as well as a daily driver, Bill Niekamp decided to build a pure salt shaker. Bill, on the right in the checkered shirt, used Harold Petersen's 364-cubic inch Chrysler motor with a 3/16-inch over bore, big valves, Potvin cam and Hilborn injection to power his 1927 T. With George Bently behind the wheel, the car clocked a two-way average of 203 miles per hour that smashed the previous record by 27 miles per hour.

SEPTEMBER 1957

In an issue containing several nice cars, including the Barris *Kopper Kart* and Larry Watson's 1950 Chevy (on the cover but no feature), Bob McCoy's flamed 1940 coupe was relegated to just one page. The flame job, radical for the time, was applied by Ray Cook of San Diego, California, who also built the nerf bars. The car was lowered by using a combination of dropped axle, 4-inch long shackles, reversed-eye spring and the removal of one leaf. Pinstriping was equally wild for 1956.

SEPTEMBER 1957

Featured on the cover to illustrate a story about how to lower your car the right way, but not featured inside, was Larry Watson's stunning 1950 Chevy. Shown here in the second of three versions, with model Elaine Sterling, Larry's *Grapevine* featured reworked A-arms, a C'd frame front and rear and dearched springs. Notice also that the grille surround was molded to the body, and the grille was fitted with 17 teeth—Larry was all smiles.

OCTOBER 1957

One of the three cover shots for the September 1957 issue was of Lloyd Bakan's 1932 three-window. With a fully detailed undercarriage, white nylon top insert and a 1954 DeSoto swap, this Deuce coupe was one of the cleanest in Los Angeles. The engine featured an Isky cam, Weiand four-carb manifold and oversize JE pistons.

'58

JULY 1958

Described as, "A familiar, often disrupting element on the starting grid of the California Sports Car Club," Duffy Livingstone's C Modified Class T/Corvette had those roundy-round guys tearing their hair out. Powered by a 1955 'Vette motor backed by a 1937 Cad trans and a 1941 Ford rear axle, this backyard bomb often beat Ferraris and Porsches. The *Eliminator* was recently purchased by author Brock Yates and was restored by Pete Chapouris' SO-CAL Speed Shop.

SEPTEMBER 1958

While streamlining for drag racing has enjoyed many proponents over the years, few have reaped the benefits and for the most part, fuelers continue to expose their wheels. In 1958, the Baron's Racing Team of Amarillo, Texas, campaigned Jack Moss' twin-Chevy-engined streamliner *2-Much*. With a sleek fiberglass body by Del Torrance, *2-Much* sported 704 inches of Corvette power pushing the envelop through the quarter in 9.67 seconds at 149 miles per hour. The car won its class at the Southern Invitational Championship.

OCTOBER 1958

The cover of the October 1958 issue featured Richard Peters' *Ala Kart*. Built by Barris Kustom on a 1929 Ford roadster pickup, *Ala Kart* won the America's Most Beautiful Roadster Award at the Oakland Roadster Show in 1958 and 1959. While being measured for a model by AMT, the Dodge Hemi-powered truck caught fire and had to be extensively rebuilt. *Ala Kart* still exists, however; in 1987 Howdy Leadbetter replicated it.

NOVEMBER 1958
With an entry list of 500 competition cars and a total turnout of some 70,000 people, the 1958 National Championship Drag Races, known as "The Big Go" were a definite hit at the Oklahoma City fairgrounds. Hot shoe of the meet was Ted Cyr (inset) who was driving two cars in the A dragster class—a tricky feat if you come up against yourself in the final. While Ted hoped to win with the new blown Chrysler orange car, which posted low elapsed time of the meet at 9.56 seconds, he did, in fact, win the meet with his old car.

DECEMBER 1958

Hot Rod's editorial mix, in the 1950s at least, was all-encompassing. For example, in the December 1958 issue, Karl Ludvigsen reported from Monza, Italy, on the new breed of Ferrari Grand Prix racers. Here is Mike Hawthorn's V-12 mount. Sporting 250 inches, six two-throat Webers and 400 horsepower, the prancing horse managed to clock 175.7 miles per hour. Despite the Indy experience in 1952, when World Champion Alberto Ascari retired after 40 laps with a broken wheel, Ferrari was still running wire wheels six years later.

JULY 1959
Featured on the cover of the July 1959 issue was Harley Earl's last car. Built by GM's engineering staff for Earl's personal use after his retirement, this Oldsmobile dream roadster, the F-88-III, featured a tubular frame with Olds suspension and an experimental Olds V-8 fitted with side-draught Webers to accommodate the low hood line. With much evidence of European styling, the car also featured an electronically retractable hardtop.

AUGUST 1959
A consistent feature of *Hot Rod* editorial since the beginning has been coverage of drag racing. In August 1959 *Hot Rod* covered the Dragons Car Club of Santa Maria, California, and its annual event at the Municipal Airport. Shown here, on the right, is Pete Capavilla of Santa Barbara in his front-blown, Chevy-powered A Roadster, which won its class.

SEPTEMBER 1959
A family that rods together, stays together. Whether that's true or not is inconsequential, but "The Draggin' Carrisosas" showed both a high degree of unity and a winning streak. Father Denny won his first trophy in 1954, and in 1959 the family pit crew watched him clock a 12-second flat run to collect his 160th trophy. Daughter Debbie races the quarter-midget, and wife Margie has also added to the collection.

OCTOBER 1959

Photographed for the cover of the October 1959 issue, John Geraghty's *Grasshopper* was built for both show and go. Geraghty (back to camera) and John Crawford of Geraghty Automotive, Eagle Rock, California, spent $3,000 and just two months creating their 1923 T-based rod. Powered by a 4-71-blown 461-inch Olds motor mated to a 1937 LaSalle trans, this bucket o' chrome ran the quarter at speeds of over 130 miles per hour.

DECEMBER 1959

Described as, "The man, the car, and the crew most likely to succeed the World's Fastest," Mickey Thompson's *Challenger I* was featured on the cover of the December 1959 issue. With four engines, Mickey set 16 records, four in each of the following distances: 5 kilometer, 345.33 miles per hour; 5 mile, 340.70 miles per hour; 10 kilometer, 327.59 miles per hour; and 10 mile, 286.16 miles per hour.

THE SIXTIES

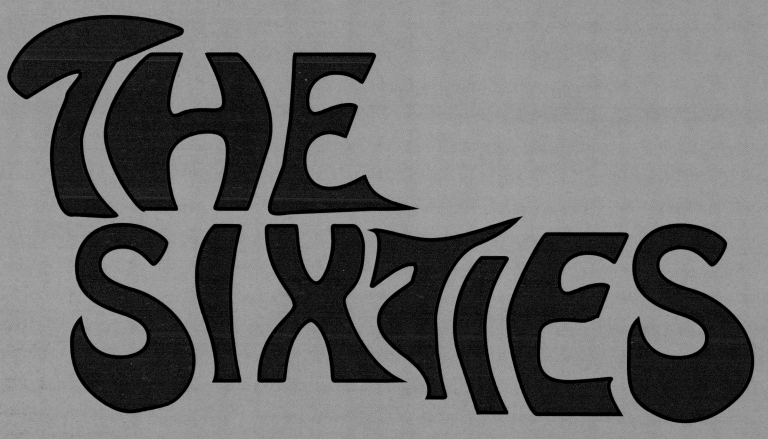

NOVEMBER 1967
One of the most competitive drivers running the Funny circuit was Gas Ronda. Though his previous mount was topping 170 with mid-eight-second elapsed times, Gas knew he could do better. The result was this Exhibition Engineering-built, glass-bodied, 1968 'Stang powered by a Hilborn-injected, Ed Pink-built SOHC Ford. It was designed to run in the sevens.

Chapter 2

Hot Rodding Heats Up

Perhaps the most turbulent era in the history of hot rodding, the 1960s represented a period of unprecedented growth and experimentation. Hot rodding embraced the full spectrum of automotive expressionism— ingenuity, performance, and genuine craziness—reflecting the unrest that characterized contemporary 1960s society. *Hot Rod* mirrored the rapidly expanding automotive enthusiasm of those times.

Tremendous strides were taken in all forms of automotive competition, and *Hot Rod* was always there to record and preserve any and all contributions to the sport's rich history. Bonneville racing and the pursuit of the Land Speed Record were always hot topics, and the battles between Mickey Thompson, the Summers Brothers, Art Arfons and Craig Breedlove are the legends upon which this sport were built.

On the drag strips, it was a similar story. If one engine was good, two were better, and four just made even more sense. The term "Funny Car" was born, but its definition was anything but a joke, and the genre developed into one of the most awesome spectacles in motorsports.

At the other end of the spectrum, there were some weird, if not downright funny lookin' cars emanating on the show circuit and from the minds of men like Ed Roth (Big Daddy). Cars like the Beatnik Bandit, which was named after, well, a beatnik bandit Roth had read about in the newspaper. Meanwhile, hot rods were cleaning up in France at the annual 24 Hours du Le Mans, where the GT40 dominated, but getting the proverbial kicked out of them in their own brickyard, when Jim Clark, Lotus and Ford put an end to the front-engine Offy era.

'60

JULY 1960
Richard Peters had won the Oakland
Roadster Show two years running, in
1958 and 1959, with the *Ala Kart*.
However, he bowed out in 1960 to give
brother-in-law Chuck Krikorian a chance
in another Barris-built car. With a fully
chromed, Krikorian-built 1931 Model-A
frame, detailed 1957 Cad motor, a Barris-
sculptured 1929 roadster body, and
custom-built grille, Chuck took home the
nine-foot AMBR trophy.

JULY 1960

At the other end of the sport, where performance was everything and looks were secondary, H. L. and N. J. Harrell of Harrell Engines, Los Angeles, fielded this record-holding 1929 roadster. Driven by Don Reynolds or Willie Borsch, who would go on to find fame with one hand on the wheel of a AA/Fuel Altered, this roadster was strictly business. Eight Stromberg 48s sat atop a 4-71 GMC blower, which was Howard-chain driven from the 412-inch Chrysler's crank. The car held numerous track records, and in the spring of 1960 set a new top speed of 144 miles per hour at LADS in Long Beach.

AUGUST 1960

The cover of the August 1960 issue was a potpourri of typical *Hot Rod* images, including Tony La Mesa's Deuce roadster. Tony, a rodder for 25 years and a member of the L.A. Roadsters, decided, according to the intro, to show up the imports and build a real American sports car. Severely channeled and fitted with a 1956 Corvette motor, it surely fitted the bill and won many trophies, although for shows rather than road racing.

OCTOBER 1960

First run in the early 1950s with a Ford engine, the yellow two-tank streamliner of Howard Johansen made two more Bonneville meets with a 1952 DeSoto before being retired. The big news in 1960 was that Howard planned a return "as-salt" scheduled for 1961 with small-block Chevy power, both blown and unblown. This ingenious device, with engine in the left pod and driver in the right, was a great promotional vehicle for Howard's Automotive, maker of speed equipment.

NOVEMBER 1960

Hot rods and teenagers were always good subjects for Hollywood exploitation movies, and in 1960 *Hot Rod* reviewed *The Choppers*. The plot placed the relatively rich boy, played by Aarch Hall Jr., as a leader of a gang of boys who specialized in stripping cars and then selling the parts to a disreputable junk yard. It sounds all too familiar. Aarch's T-bucket was, in fact, the famous Tommy Ivo bucket, at the time owned by Bill Rolland.

DECEMBER 1960

A little grainy and a little blurred, but important because it shows the new Dragmaster *Two-Thing*, which won the Best Engineered Car Award, presented by *Motor Trend*, and Top Speed of meet (171.10 miles per hour) presented by *Hot Rod*. The meet was, of course, the 1960 National Drag Championships, held over the Labor Day weekend at the Detroit Dragway. On the previous weekend, *Two-Thing* ran 180.72, and its lowest elapsed time was 9.24 seconds. Other big names of the future at that event included Jack Chrisman in the Howard Cam twin-Chevy and Eddie Hill with his Pontiac-powered rail.

'61

FEBRUARY 1961

The cover blurb said, "Customize your car with 3rd dimension paint." Of course, *Hot Rod* was talking about Metalflake paint. To get an understanding of this new product from the Dobeckmun Co., a division of Dow Chemical, *Hot Rod* went to visit, among others, Dean Jeffries, where the staff checked out Dick Scritchfield's recently 'flaked roadster. People seeing the glittering finish for the first time couldn't believe it and just had to touch.

MARCH 1961
Hot Rod called it the "Zaniest Rod Craze." Perhaps it was, but this couple, A. P. Linn and his wife from Santa Maria, California, don't look too wild behind the wheel of their flathead Cadillac-powered Ford chassis. Rims were 12-inch all around but ran only a few pounds of air. The location was Pismo Beach, where the dune riders raced up and down the 150- to 200-foot dunes.

AUGUST 1961

Hot Rod magazine and Californians have always had a fascination with racing south of the border. Down Mexico way, they definitely do it differently, and in 1961 *Hot Rod* ventured south to cover the Second Annual *Internacional Grand Prix de Tecate*— the roughest, toughest kart campaign in the world, where a 100-mile bash was won by foot! Run through the streets of this Baja border town with little or no safety structures, here you can see the infamous Tecate Club Roundhouse, with Jim Yamane driving inside Bill Woolard, who came second in "C" Class in his Go Kart.

SEPTEMBER 1961

When people think of hill climbing, they think of Pikes Peak but back in the 1960s, Model T Ford enthusiasts used to race their Tin Lizzies up Shell Hill near Signal Hill, California. Organized by the Long Beach Model T Club, the annual event in its fifth year, attracted nearly 100 entrants. They raced singly up the 1/10-mile, 22 percent course. Here, Chris Reimuller raced his Frontenac-powered car to the best time of the day, 9.861 seconds. On a chassis dyno, the motor developed 60 horsepower at 3,500 rpm.

OCTOBER 1961

In October 1961, *Hot Rod* said, "It's easy to go quick with a blower and buckets of rocker arm cubes, but Hill Alcala prefers the hard way. Raced all over California, the car, built originally by Creighton Hunter, became a family pet with Hill's wife and daughter handling the maintenance. With a 296-inch 1948 Merc motor, the car ran consistently around 130 miles per hour with 10.98 elapsed times, and performed well enough for Hill to be offered the wheel job on Dean Moon's latest dragster.

'62

JANUARY/MARCH 1962

In the search for ever more performance, the word aerodynamics entered the *Hot Rod* lexicon. In the January 1962 issue, *Hot Rod* visited Art Center College of Design student Steve Swaja, who was moonlighting at home designing bodies for So-Cal rod builders. The story precipitated a series of articles, "Adventures in Aerodynamics." Two months later, *Hot Rod* looked as far afield as Turin, Italy, where carrozzeria Ghia had developed the IXG, an 800-pound, 58-cubic Austin-Healey-powered streamliner, to attack drag and top speed records. Developed using a scale wind tunnel model, it was technically far in advance of American counterparts.

JULY 1962

In a story titled "Drags With A Twist," freelance contributor Pete Biro visited the San Francisco Region SCCA Annual Mother Lode Hill Climb. Here, gathered around the start line, are a bunch of extremely desirable sports cars, including Corvettes, Austin-Healeys, an MGA, XKE and a Porsche 356. The climb covered two miles of twisting road with 19 major turns. Top time of the meet went to Ron Hanford of Redding, California, driving a BMC Formula Junior, which covered the distance in 1:57:4.

FEBRUARY 1962

"Everybody's Automotive Magazine" as *Hot Rod* was subtitled for many years, covered all aspects of the wide world of motorsports, including road racing. Of course, in the case of Max Balchowsky's home-brewed specials, they enjoyed a kinship with traditional hot rods that could not be ignored. Here, the Mark III version of *Ol' Yaller,* with Bob Drake behind the wheel, negotiates a makeshift circuit in Pomona, California. Jack Sutton rolled out the aggressive, Ferrari-style pontoon body, while a 1960 Buick fitted with six Chevy Rochesters provided the motivation.

SEPTEMBER 1962
Mickey Thompson seemed to have his hand in everything, including the Factory Experimental class. *Hot Rod* said Factory Experimental was " . . . beginning to grab off a large share of the spotlight, with attention from fans, participants and automobile manufacturers." Thompson's *Tornado* was one of the first F/X cars to be built and quickly became the leading national contender of the AF/X class. With quarter-miles covered in 12.22 seconds and speeds like 117.27 miles per hour, the Tempest was powered by a 421 Super Duty motor fitted with Thompson aluminum rods and a Number 11 McKeller factory experimental cam.

Hot Rod Technical Editor Ray Brock got to drive almost all of the new production cars that came on the scene during his tenure at the magazine and most of them, with a few exceptions, were rather forgettable. One of the exceptions was the Cobra, seen here being driven at Riverside Raceway by Bill Krause. Brock describe the original AC-Bristol as "one of the better production cars for years in American sports car races." Even though underpowered with the 120-inch Bristol engine, the Cobra managed to trounce Corvettes regularly until the late 1950s, when growing power gave the 'Vette an edge. Of course, Shelby went on to give his Cobra an even more potent bite.

SEPTEMBER 1962

Indoor midget racing was a popular pastime in 1962. *Hot Rod* covered the scene with a visit to the 14th annual running of the BCRA (Bay Cities Racing Association) Pacific Coast Indoor Midget Championship held on a 1/10th-mile asphalt oval in the Exposition Building, Oakland, California. The standing-room-only crowd witnessed the beginning-of-the-end of Offy and Ford V-8-60 dominance, as new compact-engined midgets powered by Chevy, Ford and Buick engines took to the track. Needless to say, the 12 nights of racing provided an exciting spectacle.

'63

JANUARY 1963

It had been happening since its introduction in 1955, and by the early 1960s everybody was swapping out their flathead Ford in favor of a small-block Chevy. Eric Rickman photographed Duane Lindebaum and Don Grant dropping a triple-jugged "Mighty Mouse" into Don's 1929 A Tudor for the cover of the January issue. Unfortunately, the first set of photographs didn't turn out, and the pair had to repeat the task a few days later.

OCTOBER 1963
In the 1960s, two high-profile hot rod clubs, the Bay Area Roadsters and the L.A. Roadsters, would get together at some central location once a year. Here, associate editor Le Roi Smith (Tex) captures the action around the pool in Fresno.

SEPTEMBER 1963
The cover of the September issue featured a Bob D'Olivo action shot of upholsterer Tony Nancy's new Plymouth-powered dragster. Fitted with a 426 Plymouth stroked to 482 by Crankshaft Co., the 1,280-pound rail ran, at the time, a best of 180.72 miles per hour in 8.42 seconds. It won the coveted Best Engineered trophy at the 1963 Winternationals.

NOVEMBER 1963
Eric Rickman captured these two classic front-engined double-A rails for the cover of the November issue during the ninth annual National Championship Drag Races in Indianapolis. Top Eliminator was Phil Hobbs and runner up was Don Garlits (Big Daddy).

NOVEMBER 1963
Bob Greene wrote in the November issue that the SCTA's 15th Annual Speedfest was the biggest, most exciting in history, with single-engined streamliners hitting over 300 miles per hour, open-wheeled lakesters running at 280, and production sedans crowding 200. Fastest D/Sports Racer was this glass-bodied, Kurtis-framed 'Vette of Jack Lufkin and Denny Jones, which ran a best of 193.441 miles per hour, and set a record of 187.659 miles per hour.

'64

JANUARY 1964

Eric Rickman snapped this photo of "TV" Tommy Ivo driving the C-T Strokers digger at the LADS strip in Long Beach for a 20-page dragster special. Always the perfect "show" man, Tommy put on a heck of a display, as he powered down on Rick who was standing in the middle of the track. The car regularly ran in the seven-second bracket.

MAY 1964

The Smokers Club of Bakersfield presented the annual U.S. Fuel and Gas Championship, which was often, and rightly, referred to as the "dragster showdown." Here, "Big Daddy" Don Garlits in the *Wynns Jammer* looked to be a little late off the line but went through to the finals only to lose to Connie Kalitta in the *Bounty Hunter*. Connie pulled a 7.95 for low elapsed time of the 3-day meet.

FEBRUARY 1964

Looking for other avenues of income, the Dragmaster Company of Carlsbad, California, introduced the "instant" roadster and invited the staff of *Hot Rod* to watch them "Build a Roadster in a Day." In fact, the car was actually built for Wally Parks, president of the NHRA. In all, the 1927 T-bodied, tube-framed, Cobra-powered roadster took just 6 hours, 50 minutes and 11 seconds to assemble.

MAY 1964

Two-wheeled drag racing has always been a heart-stopping concept, and it was no less in the 1960s. One of the big guys of the day was Pasadenan Clem Johnson and his immaculate *Barn Job*. Powered by a British Vincent H. R. D. V-twin pumped up from 61 to 85 cubic inches, Clem clipped the quarter in 9.82 seconds at 151.51 miles per hour.

MAY 1964

For the cover of the May issue, Rick photographed Dean Jeffries' phenomenal *Manta Ray*. The *Manta Ray*'s Jeffries-formed aluminum body was sculpted atop a prewar Maserati Grand Prix racing car chassis fitted with a Weber-fueled Cobra motor. At the time, nobody wanted an old race car. Dean stills owns the car.

MAY 1964

Hot Rod never covered much rallying, but in 1964, Mercury entered four specially prepared Super Cyclone Comets in the 12th East African Safari. Only about 100 miles of the 3,100-mile route through Kenya, Uganda and Tanganyika was on paved roads, but under the direction of Team Manager Don Franciso, the 289-powered Comets fared well.

MAY 1965
Fred Marasco looks wistfully out over the ocean as he leans against the Cal Auto fiberglass body of his 1923 T roadster pickup, which graced the cover of the May issue. Fred, a member of the Bay Area Roadster Club, built a traditional-looking T with a host of unusual details. For example, a high-performance F-85 Olds nestled between the engined-turned rail covers, while the chassis sported four-bar links and torsion-bar front suspension and quad coil-overs on the rear.

MAY 1965

K. S. Pitman's 1933 Willy's A/Gas coupe was one of the all-time crowd pleasers. Holding nearly every elapsed time and top speed record, Pitman topped his year with a win at the NHRA's Indy Nationals. The team even went to England as part of the U.S. Drag Team. The car was very consistent, running the quarter in 9.70 seconds at 151 miles per hour.

JUNE 1965

"New car by an old pro," was how *Hot Rod* described Bonneville basher Bill Burke's latest salt shaker. Photographed here for the cover of the June issue, Bill could be seen dropping in the front-mounted, Potvin-blown, Hilborn-injected 1,066-horsepower 450-cubic inch Chrysler, which he expected would push into the record books. Briggs Cunningham, George Hurst and the Reynolds Aluminum Company all supported Bill's effort. Incidentally, Dick Dean handled the tin bashing.

JULY 1965
Weight transfer were the watch words of the 1960s, and Jack Charisman's 427-powered Comet took the notion to the extreme with its motor pushed all the way back (25 percent) into the interior and "Smiling Jack" jammed up against the rear window. Jack's car was the basic FX drag package, complete with fiberglass hood, fenders and doors, along with plastic windows. Now what are the chances of there being any new old stock out there in a quiet Mercury dealership?

OCTOBER 1965
An engineering colloquialism says to "put some English on it," and in the 1960s gasser wars small, short-wheelbase, light-weight English bodies such as the 1948 four-door Prefect used on George (Ohio George) Montgomery's *Hurst's Gasser Passer* were all the rage. Can you believe a stock frame was raised on parallel leaf springs and powered by a blown 350 Chevy?

AUGUST 1965
"Streamlining-Dragster Dilemma" was the headline for August's cover story which featured Connie Kalitta's double-A fueler, photographed by Bob D'Olivo in Ford's 140-mile per hour wind tunnel. While the drag racers did learn that aerodynamics were an important aspect of race car design, the full-bodied experiments of the 1960s were just that—experiments.

JANUARY 1966
The Bonneville Salt Flats had, the previous year, seen almighty action as a host of rocket men like Art and Walt Arfon, Craig Breedlove, the Summers Brothers, and Bob Tatroe battled it out for the land speed record. Lower down the charts, Red Holmes and Jerry Kugel used a 260-cubic inch Ford to push a brick of a Deuce roadster down that long black line for a new E/GR record of 163.350 miles per hour. Jerry and his sons eventually ran a similar roadster well past the 200-mile per hour mark before retiring it.

↑

JULY 1966
The cover of the July issue saw Eric Rickman capture Don Edmunds power sliding this Super Modified kit car at Ascot park, Gardena, California For $3,550 you got everything except paint, chrome, engine, tires, upholstery and plumbing, which is all the expensive parts. Nobody ever said racing was cheap.

JULY 1966
"It can't last." That's what they all said about the funny cars when they first began to make their presence felt on the nation's drag strips. Time has proved the nay sayers wrong, and one of those who kept the fire burning was Charlie Allen and his Atlantic Dodge-sponsored 1966 Dart. A 426 Hemi pushed this not-so-funny car to 9.34 at 148.20 miles per hour.

JULY 1966

Dodge didn't have it all their own way in 1966. Take, for example, Bruce Larson's 1966 Chevelle. Front wheels were pushed forward 4 inches, rear wheels 12, hub caps replaced the headlights, steering gear was, from all things, a 1963 Corvair, and the motor was a ram-tubed, Hilborn-injected 454 running on nitro and alky.

AUGUST 1966

While T buckets were mostly of the 1923 Ford variety, Fresno, California, carpenter Joe Hill went a different route with a $20 1917 Dodge touring body that he had cut down to roadster size. Dodge or no Dodge, power was provided by the ubiquitous small-block 283 Chevy, in this case fitted with Joe-carved wooden valve and carb covers.

NOVEMBER 1966
The follow-up to the infamous Grand-Spaulding eight-second 1965 match car was this 1,850-pound Super-Charger of "Mr. Norm." Here, driver Gary Dyer and "Mr. Norm" Kraus discuss the potential of the 1966 car. The car was projected to run high sevens in the low 190s. Not unlikely since the glass Charger body weighed a mere 220 pounds, and the chassis just 250 pounds.

APRIL 1967
By the mid-1960s, the way-out show rod fad was in full bloom. One of the genre's best exponents was Ray Farhner of Kansas City. Based on a horse drawn hearse built by Cunningham of New York in the mid-1800s, Ray's *Boothill Express* was one of the better examples. The coach body was installed on a 2x4 box tube frame and fitted with a 500-horse Hilborn-injected Chrysler.

APRIL 1967
Though not a show rod per se, Phil Kendrick's Deuce Tudor won the Grand Sweepstakes Award at the 1967 San Mateo Auto Show—first time out. Sitting just right for the times, Phil chopped his sedan 4 inches and bobbed the rear fenders and moved the gas tank to where the back seat used to be. Tony Del Rio sprayed the 40 coats of orange and "Tommy the Greek" handled the striping.

JULY 1967

Cover car for the July issue was the side-by-side Pontiac-powered *Invader* roadster of Bob Reisner. Bob built this twin-engined rod with two goals in mind: To get on the Cover of *Hot Rod* magazine and to win the America's Most Beautiful Roadster Award at the National Roadster Show. He succeeded in his dream and won many other trophies besides. Besides two engines, *Invader* also had twin B&M stick hydros and twin Jaguar rear ends.

AUGUST 1967

Photographed by Eric Rickman outside Dean Moon's shop where Fred Larsen works, the Larsen and Cummins streamliner had but one purpose, and that was to go fast and straight. At the time, with a front-mounted, blown, 180-inch small-small-block Chevy, it ran 225 miles per hour.

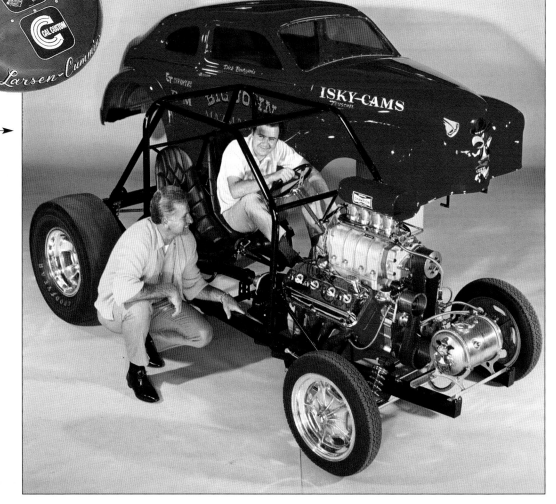

SEPTEMBER 1967

Small English sedans continued to be the bodies of choice in the gasser classes, and for the cover of the September 1966 issue John Mazmanian (Big John) showed off his latest. Fitted with a fiberglass two-door Austin, the car was said to be "detailed to perfection." With a 3/4-inch C-T stroker kit, the Dave Zeuschel-built 1957 Chrysler Hemi was upped to 427 inches.

'68

JANUARY 1968
The January 1968 issue was a special anniversary issue celebrating 20 years of hot rodding. Featured in that issue was "Dandy Dick" Landy's 1968 team, which consisted of his brother Mike (left) and this pair of 1968 Dodge Chargers running in the increasingly popular "professional" Top Stock class. Landy participated in the Dodge Performance Clinics.

MARCH 1968
Bob D'Olivo captured Dan Gurney winning the first Rex Mays 300. Gurney, of course, still campaigns under the All American Racers banner.

FEBRUARY 1968
Photographed for the cover by Pat Broiler was Ronnie Sox, who gathered data that was passed on to thousands of enthusiasts through the Sox and Martin Plymouth Performance Clinics. Running in Super Stock, the "A" car was powered by a Plymouth 440 wedge coupled to a four-speed trans.

APRIL 1968
In 1968, John Dianna wasn't even employed by Petersen Publishing when his 1956 Sedan Delivery was featured on the cover. Today he is president of the Automotive Performance Group. A past H/Stock champion, John built his wagon to run in the increasingly popular "Jr. Stock" class and even assembled the engine himself. Maiden run at the 1968 Winternationals netted a 14.38 elapsed time at 95.44 miles per hour.

JULY 1969

For the most part, *Hot Rod* magazine left the roundy-round stuff to other magazines. A fast car, however, is a fast car. Here are three of the fastest during the 1969 running of the Daytona 24 Hours. From left to right it was Vic Elford in a Porsche 908, Jo Bonnier and Mark Donohue both in Lola T-70s. Bob D'Olivo snapped the shutter.

MAY 1969
Pat Broiler captured Bill Jenkins (Grumpy) accelerating hard toward another victory in the Super Stock ranks in his Camaro, *Grumpy's Toy.*

AUGUST 1969
Tom McEwen (The Mongoose) was one of several drivers campaigning both a dragster and a Funny Car in 1969. Here, Don Prieto captured the "'Goose" for the *Hot Rod* Racing Gallery while shoeing his direct-drive Barracuda.

JUNE 1969
Connie Kalitta was one of the first to drop a SOHC motor into a dragster and he was obviously impressed because for the 1969 season he ran not one but two Ford 429 "twisted Hemi" powered *Bounty Hunters*, his dragster and a new funny car. Two-car teams were all the rage in 1969.

←

AUGUST 1969

More often than not, show cars inspired plastic models, but occasionally it happened the other way. Such was the case of the *Red Baron*. Conceived as a humorous variation for model builders by designer Tom Daniel, the 1/24-scale Monogram Model prompted show promoter Bob Larivee to build a full-size replica right down to the chrome-plated twin Spandau machine guns. Originally, Daniel had specified a Mercedes airplane engine but when none could be found, builder Chuck Miller settled for a OHC Pontiac six.

NOVEMBER 1969

"The salt was fine in '69" said the headline of coverage of the 21st Annual Bonneville National Speed Trials. On the cover was this Eric Rickman photograph of the Peek Bros. B/Gas Roadster. Brothers Jerry and Greg both got into what was then called the Iskenderian 200 miles per hour Club with a best two-way average of 209.250 miles per hour.

THE SEVENTIES

SEPTEMBER 1971
People often have a tendency to
like the underdog and to root for the
David in his battle with Goliath. Perhaps
that's why they liked *Inch Pincher Too* so much.
EMPI started drag racing the diminutive Bug back in 1965
and did very well, but their new I/Gasser, introduced in 1971,
reflected all the very latest technology. Based on a 1959 sunroof
sedan, the little car that would was powered by a 123-inch 1971 motor
mated to a '59 Porsche transaxle. Shakedown times were in the high 11-second
range, but it eventually went much faster.

Chapter 3

Making the Best of It

Hot Rod continued to maintain a high profile throughout the 1970s by inspiring the sport, rather than just reporting on it. A total of six editors carved and sculptured the appearance and involvement of Hot Rod in this decade. Don Evans was a carryover shoe-in from the previous decade until he relinquished his position to A. B. Shuman. After Arnold completed the March 1972 issue, Terry Cook took charge for over two years, before leading Jim McCraw to the hot seat. John Dianna picked up where Jim left off in February 1986 and continued to climb the corporate ladder, opening the door for the decade's final editor, Lee Kelley.

Among the many topics featured in the 1970s were a host of editorials designed to provoke reader response over increasing governmental regulation, the van craze (from conception to public dissent), the hot rodder's better idea—V-8 in a Vega, Shirley Muldowney's climb to Top Fuel fame, Bill Jenkins' bare skin rug color centerfold, and the evolution of Street Freak machines to Pro Street masterpieces. For the dedicated 1970s hot rodder, Hot Rod was the best source for the sport's news and views.

Bracket racing became extremely popular in the mid-1970s since it allowed any racer to "run what he brung." While safety was still a prime concern, engine, weight, and modification rules were relaxed, providing a competitive drag racing outlet for any car no matter how fast or slow it was. The handicap-based system may have been confusing at first, but after Hot Rod published a few tips and how-to articles on the subject, racers flocked to the strip in hopes of lucrative purses.

Hot Rod's biggest bracket racing support came with the August 1977 introduction of the new series titled "Bracket Racing America." This ongoing feature spotlighted the sport as it grew throughout the country. Each month, Hot Rod showcased quarter-mile tracks and race cars that were currently participating in the program. This support obviously paid off.

MARCH 1970

For most people, it was a facet of the hot rod sport they would never be able to see, let alone participate in. However, for those who lived in southern California, two nearby areas of sand dunes, Pismo Beach and Glamis, provided space where the sport of dune buggying could be enjoyed. In the beginning, the buggies were nothing more than stripped-down Model T and A Fords, but as the sport matured, more sophisticated machinery appeared. With the VW Beetle, the desert rats found the perfect powerplant. The V-Dub boxer engine, lightweight and air-cooled, remains the engine of choice, mounted in the rear or reversed and mounted amidships. Even today, at Thanksgiving, more than 100,000 make the trek to Glamis to kick some sand.

APRIL 1970

Amid major tire wars between Firestone and Goodyear, sister magazine *Motor Trend* sponsored the eighth running of the Riverside 500, reported upon in the April 1970 issue. Staring from 35th position, Parnelli Jones moved up to 18th in the first lap, to 9th after six laps and to 2nd on lap 20. In the lead, during lap 169, P. J.'s clutch went out and A. J. Foyt took the lead in his 1970 Ford—finally collecting first place money at a track that had not been good to him before.

SEPTEMBER 1970
Of all the wildest five-wheelers ever featured in the pages of *Hot Rod*, Tom McMullen's *Big Twin* beats all. Tom, who ran one of the baddest black n' flamed highboy roadsters ever and went on to form his own publishing company, was, at the time, operating AEE Choppers in Anaheim, California, where he built *Big Twin* as a promotional tool. It certainly was an attention grabber and took his second-in-a-row Motorcycle Sweepstakes win at the 1969 Oakland Roadster Show. The bike? Trike? Quike? Call it what you will, it ran two Harley 883 Sportster motors, one with reversed heads, a Ford C4 trans and a Harley-Davidson Servicar rear axle driven through a transfer shaft. The paint was, of course, by Molly.

OCTOBER 1970
Everything, even street rods, was influenced by the drag strip-oriented muscle car scene, and John Aleman, of Chandler, Arizona, was one of the afflicted. With a roll bar and sans mufflers, John's blown 430-cubic inch 1961 Lincoln-motored 1923 T managed a sub-10-second quarter at a healthy 9.73 seconds. And, when the dust cleared, he could drive this puppy home.

DECEMBER 1970
Geez! How'd that happen? As he was launching, the rear end supports on Eldon Huffman's Funny Car broke. The slick caught the underside of the body and in half a second, it rearranged the aerodynamics of Huff's Charger.

MARCH 1971

While Detroit was busy downsizing, hot rodders were equally busy stretching them out and narrowing them down. Huff & Saunders' Vega was stretched 20 inches and narrowed 5 inches to fit the dimensions of a competitive flopper frame. A former NHRA Winternationals champ, Clare Saunders liked to thrill the crowd with smoky burnouts and 40-mile per hour backups to the starting line, which kept the start line crew on its toes. Running out of New Orleans with a Frank Huff-built 454 rat motor and a 27-percent overdriven blower, the viscous Vega cranked out some impressive quarters, with times around 7.17 seconds and speeds in excess of 206 miles per hour.

APRIL 1971
The April 1971 issue focused on the so-called Super All-Star Funny Car Scene, which dominated the sport at that time. However, Keeling, Clayton, and Ramsey were the names on everybody's lips after the inaugural Supernationals at Ontario Motor Speedway. Those who worked on this beautiful *California Charger* digger read like a Who's Who of drag racing. The *California Charger* sported a 210-inch chassis by Don Long, tin bending by Tom Hanna and Ken Ellis, paint by George Cerny, and upholstery by Tony Nancy.

JULY 1971

Zingers? Could be a cereal, could be a Saturday morning cartoon but, in fact, they were the idea of Dennis Johnson, who entered a model of such in the Detroit Autorama's model car contest. The product planners at Model Products Corporation (MPC) saw Dennis' efforts and decided to put a line into production. Next, Bob Larivee, of Group Promotions thought that full-size Zingers would be real crowd pleasers for his International Championship Auto Shows, so he commissioned Chuck Miller and Steve Tansy to enlarge upon MPC's theme. Besides the two 'Vettes shown, there was a VW Beetle, a dune buggy, and a Dodge Van.

OCTOBER 1971

Cover car for the September 1971 issue was Gary and Jerry Mallicoat's twice-turbocharged Chrysler Hemi-powered 1969 Barracuda, which ran in BB/A or AA/GS class at NHRA events. Turbocharging was the word on everybody's lips when driver Tom Chambliss set a new BB/A record of 172.08 miles per hour, far surpassing the old 165.74-mile per hour mark. Elapsed time was 8.6 seconds but the team planned to "lean on the motor" and get into the 8.30s. At the time, Hilborn was offering a turbo kit for the 392 Chrysler.

DECEMBER 1971

The headline said, "When is a street roadster not a street roadster?" When it's Tony Del Rio's show-winning, record-setting, Chevy-powered flip-top." Breaking away from his Willys and Anglia Gasser background, Tony built this glass-bodied A/Street Roadster to campaign both the track and show circuits. It certainly did well on the strip—at the NHRA Winternationals, Tony ran 9.72 seconds at 139.76 miles per hour and earned the Best Appearing Award. Power came from a Hilborn-injected 1969 Chevy big block with Cylinder Head Engineering heads, Venolia pistons, Howard rods, and a Vertex mag.

JANUARY 1972

An original investment of just $4,500, a rented one-car garage and a borrowed trailer was all that the team of John Keeling, Jerry Clayton, and Rick Ramsey started with, but by 1972 the team was fielding a top fuel dragster as well as this beautiful Pinto-bodied funny car. With a 1958 396 Chrysler New Yorker motor, this flopper evidenced all the latest safety features, including Simpson on-board fire bottles and Sperex fire-retardant paint on the underside of the body.

FEBRUARY 1972

Drag racing took a major turn with the introduction of the sport's very own engine. Developed by Ed Donovan, this all-aluminum replacement for the ubiquitous, early 392 Chrysler Hemi was designed to retain the 92's inherent advantages and cure its shortcomings. Punched out to 417 cubic inches, Donovan's motor consisted of an engine block with eight wet-sleeve cylinder liners and a separate main bearing support. Needless to say, it revolutionized drag racing. First time out, in John Wiebe's hands, the motor set a new Ontario record of 6.53 seconds.

MARCH 1972
Besides a strong complement of vans, which were the popular form of street transportation in the 70's, the March issue also featured a heavy street roadster section. Included was this great action shot by Don Emmons of Jerry Cosce's 1932 Bantam roadster. With a 327 Chevy in a shortened Model-A frame, it had all the looks of an altered, even down to the lack of front brakes.

JULY 1972
Woodys have always been popular hot rodder's fodder, and Darryl Norenberg photographed this near-perfect pair for the July issue. Owned by Jim Sadler and Tom Karp, members of The Forties Limited Inc. club, Karp's 1940 deluxe model was one of only 8,730 built, while Sadler's 1940 was a Standard model.

NOVEMBER 1972
Here's the reason behind the need for all that safety equipment. When a Funny Car's motor explodes, as it did in Kenny Goodell's ride, you need all the help you can get.

FEBRUARY 1972
Tagged "The Rumour Nationals," the NHRA's end-of-1971 Supernationals had everybody guessing what rule changes for 1972 would bring. Also, there were rumors of a possible switch to American Motors for Mr. Gasket Co.-sponsored "Dyno Don" Nicholson's Pro Stock, which ran a 9.60.

MARCH 1973

In March 1973, *Hot Rod* described Mickey Thompson as a "Speed impresario," and perhaps no other moniker suited the man better. Always innovative, he tried his hand at everything and succeeded at most things he tried. Mickey raced Funny Cars for many years and each year tried to come up with something different. In 1973 it was a Pontiac Grand Am powered by a 540-inch elephant motor riding on a Lil' John Buttera chassis with a body by Pelligrini Fiberglass. Veteran wheel man Butch Mass handled the driving chores.

FEBRUARY 1973

Jungle Jim might have been the man behind the wheel, but the woman behind the man was Jungle Pam, and she graced the cover of the February 1973 issue. Pam Hardy was actually the front woman for a funny car issue, when *Hot Rod* asked a couple of poignant questions, such as "Is the Funny Car Dead?" and "Who's This Kid Billy Meyer, and Where Does He Get Off?" Of course, time has answered both questions. Funny cars are alive and faster than ever, and it was a virtual unknown Billy who slipped in and blew everyone into the weeds to win the Orange County International Raceway Manufacturers' Funny Car Championships. At the time, Billy was an unsponsored 18-year-old.

SEPTEMBER 1973

Well-known southern California racers Jim de Frank and Andy Cohen not only shared a love of drag racing, which manifested itself in a 1968 Dodge Dart Super Stock race car, they also shared a love of hot rods, evidenced by this pair of Model As. The racer ran a 426 Hemi prepared by ace wrench Joe Allread, while their Fords, both of 1928 vintage, were quite different. Jim's roadster pickup ran a 427 L-88 big-block while Andy opted for a 365-horsepower version of the 327 small-block. Andy went on to create Beverly Hills Motoring Accessories; Jim owns California Car Cover.

SEPTEMBER 1973

At the 1973 NHRA Spring Nationals in Columbus, Ohio, Shirley Muldowney, ("Cha Cha" as she was known then) wowed the crowd by defeating Jim Murphy in Round One. Sadly, she lost in Round Two. The eventual winner was John Wiebe from Newton, Kansas, whose Sid Waterman-built Donovan stopped the clocks at 6.49, with a top speed of 226.13 miles per hour.

JANUARY 1974
The Racing Action feature in the January 1974 issue was this great Jere Alhadeff photograph, taken during the infamous Baja 500 race. Sadly, there was no information accompanying the shot, nevertheless, it's great to see an Edsel put to good use—its namesake, Edsel Ford, would be proud.

FEBRUARY 1974
Believe it or not, the interest in import mini-trucks began way back in the early 1970s with vehicles like Toyota's Yamahauler. Turbocharged by Ak Miller, the Yamahauler sported a Jaguar XKE independent rear suspension and Cragar wheels. The paint scheme in Yamaha colors was conceived and executed by Molly, who continues to be active in the conception and execution of such projects.

APRIL 1974

Los Angeles, where *Hot Rod* magazine is published, has always been regarded as a mecca and progenitor of automotive trends., "Within the monstrous urban sprawl known as Los Angeles," editor Terry Cook said, "a thousand separate subcultures are nurturing." One of those subcultures is lowriders, and one of the leading crews was the Imperials. Primarily from Whittier, but with members from all over the Los Angeles basin, the Imperials were Chicanos (a self-coined word to describe people of Mexican-American descent) with some of the coolest and lowest rides in town.

DECEMBER 1974

The name Lil' John Buttera is one that appears constantly in *Hot Rod*. As a master craftsman of the funny car movement, it was a surprise to most to find that John was equally at home building a hot rod for the street. And not any usual rod, this was a 1926 T Tudor, which first appeared in Terry Cook's "Great California Street Rod Civil War." Buttera set out to build an all-independent suspension system that would live on the street and showcase his ability to work with all types of materials. Famed drag racer Art Chrisman built the 1967 289-inch Ford, while Steve Davis handled the tin work. Although John wanted the T to appear somewhat stock on the outside, the inside was circa 1972 Caddy, down to the digital clocks, climate controls and idiot lights.

SEPTEMBER 1974
By September 1974, a young Gary Beck from Edmonton, Alberta, was making a name for himself being Twice-National Champion and running a Spring Nationals-first of 5.98 at 247.25 miles per hour. Wheelbases, like times, were already out there, as evidenced by this 230-inch Woody Gilmore example, loaded for bear with 490 inches of Keith Black aluminum elephant motor. And look at all that start line activity as Gary pulls a hole shot to win against "Large Father" Don Garlits.

MARCH 1975

In the March 1975 issue, the editors of *Hot Rod* declared that automotive magazines run on good photography, and that statement is as true today as it was back then. In visual explanation of what they meant, the March issue featured a color spread of the work of a 31-year-old Brooklyn native, Howard Koby. Howard relocated to Los Angeles and worked all the local tracks and as far afield as Pikes Peak. This fuel-altered burning out in the night was just one of his many incredible images.

APRIL 1975

Texan Roland Jiminez worked hard helping his older brother build a 427 Chevy-powered 1932 Ford, but when it came time for a turn behind the wheel, big brother was nowhere to be found. Undeterred, Roland decided his own ride was the answer, so he hooked up with Roy Thomas in San Antonio, and between them they concocted this wild brewski. A 1970 vintage 426 Chrysler Hemi, complete with Bowers magnesium blower and twin Holley 750 double-pumpers and drag-style weed spreader exhausts is only partially hidden by the Jim Babb radiator. With no windshield, crash helmets were mandatory for Roland and his girlfriend.

OCTOBER 1975

Don Thelan was one of those consummate hot rod scroungers who could ferret out vintage tin in a most uncanny way. This 1934 sedan delivery he found in the San Fernando Valley north of Los Angeles and "rodstored" it in a matter of just five months. He and Ron Jones added new wood and patch panels, while Pete Chapouris and Jim Jacobs (Jake) of Pete and Jake's reworked the original chassis to take a 289-inch Ford V-8. Don went on to build five winners of the America's Most Beautiful Roadster Award.

←

MAY 1975
Coverage of the annual Bonneville Speed Trials included the *Supercharged Stogie* of Ernie Bennet and Gil and Kenny Ruiz. It was powered by an Ak Miller turbocharged two-liter four-cylinder Ford Capri motor. The team hoped to take the G lakester record to a new high. The car, which Ernie had peddled to a 220-mile per hour run when it had been powered by a fuel-burning V-8, was shaped by Ed Kuzma and painted by Sam Foose.

JANUARY 1976

'Vettes and Vans were the subject of the cover of the January 1976 issue. While the 'Vette has matured into a world-class sports car, the van craze went the way of most fads—south! Of all the wild and crazily customized Corvettes in that issue, John Greenwood's was, without doubt, the most awesome. Tagged the world's fastest Corvette, it was clocked at speeds in excess of 230 miles per hour on Daytona's tri-oval. At the time, it was estimated that John had spent well over $125,000 developing his Trans-Am racer, in three years of development at his Troy, Michigan, shop. Replicas, less engine, trans and tires, could be had for a paltry $18,000.

MARCH 1976

Baskerville's Gallery usually evidenced some pretty wild machinery, and the March 1976 edition was no exception with well known author/publisher Holly Hedrich's low flyer. Assembled at *Modern Rod* magazine's Test Tube T, the rod/dragster/UFO (you choose) was finished by Steve Tansy and put on the show circuit.

APRIL 1976

They called it the SMI *Motivator*. *Hot Rod* called it potentially the world's fastest tricycle. Sponsored by the somewhat unusual Success Motivation Institute, the thrice-wheeled meteor was campaigned by Bill Fredrick and Billy and Paul Meyer. Billy, of course, was the fresh-faced kid who turned the drag racing world on its head in 1972 when, at the age of 16, he won the Manufacturers' Funny Car Championship at OCIR. Powered by a Romatec V4 Hydrogen Peroxide rocket system capable of producing 48,000 horsepower, the aim was 743 miles per hour.

AUGUST 1976

In another issue dominated by truckin' times, Baskerville's Gallery in August 1976 featured this highly modified 1971 Pontiac Firebird belonging to Dave Cook of Brookfield, Connecticut. Altered along the lines delineated by famed auto designer Harry Bradley, Dave's orange crush featured doors sectioned 3 inches, a raked windshield, functional multiscooped hood, flush-mounted headlights and some extremely large rear fender skirts. Candy tangerine was the color of this streamlined baby.

OCTOBER 1976

Baskerville's Gallery once again provided the meatiest part of the magazine, and in October his menu included this peek at the Pike, where this side-piped Camaro raced for the clouds.

'77

FEBRUARY 1977

Don Blair, the owner of Blair's Speed Shop, one of the original speed shops, eventually sold the enterprise to Phil Lukens. To help promote the business, Phil campaigned this monstrous *Topolino* which he purchased from Tom Shinholster of Cape Canaveral, Florida. The 1,500-pound, 900-plus horsepower mighty mouse with its Bowers shotgun-injected 341-inch Chrysler regularly ran around the 165-mile per hour vicinity.

APRIL 1977

The cover car for the April 1977 issue was Gratiot's all-new, easy-to-assemble Track-T kit. The early track roadster styling was the brain child of metal-master Ron Fornier. When he showed his concept to Gratiot, main man Angelo Giampetroni saw the commercial potential. Gratiot had sold over 100 T-bucket kits during the previous few years, and here was a racy alternative. Photographed here, on a typical Detroit winter's day, with Gray Baskerville behind the wheel and Angelo riding shotgun, the V-8 Gratiot Track-T featured a rollcage and wind-deflecting wrap-around windshield.

AUGUST 1977
Hot Rod magazine has always been known for its great project cars, and in 1976, editor John Dianna and renowned engine builder John Lingenfelter dreamed up this 3-in-1 triple-threat Chevy. Based on a 1966-67 Chevy II Nova, this rad racer competed in Modified Eliminator, Super Modified and even Super Stock classes, simply by shuffling various components. The graphics were designed by Kenny Youngblood and executed by Jack Trost.

OCTOBER 1977

By the late 1970s, hot rods, now called street rods, were regaining their earlier popularity and *Hot Rod* magazine brought its readers a multipart build-up series focused on the popular 1932 Ford roadster. Jerry Kugel (left) of Kugel Komponents handled the frame work and assembled this resto-style rod. Components came from a number of manufacturers, including Pete and Jake's Hot Rod Parts (suspension), Super Bell (front axle), and The Deuce Factory (reproduction parts).

NOVEMBER 1977

Driving the rod revival was the National Street Rod Association's Street Rod Nationals. Now attracting upwards of 10,000 rods, the Street Rod Nats was a must-drive-to event and plenty of left coasters like Pete Chapouris of Pete and Jake's Hot Rod Parts made the annual cross-country pilgrimage. Pete's black n' flamed 1934 coupe was featured in a 1974 made-for-TV movie called *The California Kid*. It helped establish Pete and Jake's as one of the premier hot rod shops.

FEBRUARY 1978

For the most part, the van thing consisted of porthole windows and acres of shag-pile carpet. Occasionally, somebody would do something a little different. One of those somebodies was famed show car builder and AMBR winner Carl Casper. *Carl's 2002 Vanturian* featured a box-tube chassis with Corvette and Olds Cutlass suspension, an extremely "cab-forward" driving position and a 6-71 huffed 454-inch rat motor. The Casper-formed fiberglass body was entered through a forward-tilting cockpit.

MAY 1978

In an issue packed with Corvettes, Corvette stuff and Corvette how-tos, Gary Meadors' mildly chopped 1932 Deuce sedan stood out as a subtle street rod with plain yellow paint and simple pin stripes but plenty of attitude. Under the hood was a stout 1967 350-inch Chevy. Gary, of course, went on to form the Goodguys Rod & Custom Association and stages street rod events all over the nation.

MAY 1978

Ever since Sam Barris chopped the first 1949 Merc sedan, the car has been the quintessential kustom. Over the years, many have tried to emulate Sam's style and few have succeeded. However, in the best 1950s tradition, Mike North of Lansing, Michigan, nosed, decked and frenched his 1951 until it was perfect. A hand-made floating-bar grille, deep Imron black by Mike Maloney, lakes pipes, Olds fiesta hub caps and fuzzy dice hanging from the rear-view mirror complete the time travel. Under the hood it was a 1952 Merc 239-inch flattie updated with a Holley carb and Offy intake.

JULY 1978

The diminutive English Anglia was forever popular in the gasser classes because of its short wheelbase, narrow track and light weight. However, by 1978, most gassers resembled Pro Stockers, so it was refreshing to see the Thames panel of Larry Buchanan and partner Mark Woznichak. Except for the one-piece glass front end, the car was all steel and powered by a Hilborn injected 13:1 open chamber 427 Chevy. It ran high eight-second elapsed times at around 156 miles per hour.

FEBRUARY 1979
"Wild Bill" Shrewsberry was the consummate crowd pleaser with his 1930 Ford
panel truck wheelstander. Sponsored by Knott's Berry Farm, Buena Park, California,
the Wild Bill show was in constant demand on the drag racing exhibition circuit.
With a steel body, no doubt plenty of weight in the rear and a blown fuel Chrysler
for power, the Berry Wagon regularly tripped the lights at speeds around the 124
miles per hour mark in the low 10-second range—and on two wheels.

MARCH 1979

The March 1979 issue contained a how-to feature on flame-painting techniques and was illustrated on the cover with three outrageous examples. On the left was Terry Berzenye's 465-horsepower Boss 351-powered three-hole Deuce. On the right it was Mel and Kathy Jeffries' immaculate 1955 Chevy Nomad, while the spotlight was taken by *Hot Rod's* very own project-to-be 1979 Plymouth Road Runner, which was used in this instance by Eddie Paul as a canvas on which he showed readers the right way to apply flames.

MAY 1979

The story was titled "The Boss is Back" and aptly described the return of Sox and Martin to professional drag racing. Following a too-long, six-year layoff that came with the withdrawal of corporate sponsorship, the dynamic duo, Ronnie and Buddy, returned to the Pro Stock ranks with Chrysler support in the form of a diminutive front-wheel-drive 1979 Omni/Horizon body, small-block 337-inch Mopar motor and Jet-X sponsorship.

AUGUST 1979

Another of *Hot Rod*'s many projects was this Total Performance T-bucket. This over-the-counter kit rod was the door prize at *Hot Rod* magazine's first annual Hot Rod Nationals. At the time, The Total T could be built for less than $5,000 and appeared to be an ideal starting point for would-be rodders.

DECEMBER 1979

The December issue was one of extremes. On the fold-out cover, Lil' John Buttera's rectangular-headlighted (they were from a Citroen 2CV) new-wave Deuce, which set a smoothie trend that lasted almost 20 years. At the other end of the spectrum was "Whistling Norm" Grabowski's Henway. (as in, "What's a Henway?" "Oh, about three or four pounds") Sporting a heavily-riveted—842 brass cap screws, to be exact—industrial look, this Tennessee stakebed rode on Corvette suspension.

THE Eighties

SEPTEMBER 1987
If for nothing else, the 1980s will be remembered for Pro Street—big tires, tubs and 10-second street cars. One of the best examples of the breed was Scott Brenner's 1969 Camaro, which was the September 1987 cover car. A blown 402-cubic inch all-aluminum, Donovan small-block with a dry sump oiling system might have been beyond the average Pro Street project, but Scott was determined to outclass the class. With 9-second capability and the looks to match, Scott's expedition to the ultimate featured a Doug Nash five-speed transmission and a Dana 60 rear end.

Chapter 4

Going in Style

Despite relatively high-priced gasoline, smog controls, CAFE standards, and complicated electronically controlled cars (a mere toggle switch when compared to what was to come), "Hot rodding," as Pat Ganahl said, "branched, blossomed, and had grown wild in the 1980s."

The most amazing thing about the 1980s was that some people thought that the automobile would be as outmoded as the horse, and motorsports would be akin to antique collecting. Just the opposite was true, although some people had begun to rediscover those hidden and almost forgotten treasures of yesteryear, and old hot rods and race cars began to appreciate like antiques.

The sport was seeing phenomenal growth in almost every quarter. Drag racing was hard on the heels of NASCAR in becoming a major, multimillion dollar sport. Hot rodding, with the arrival on the scene of Boyd Coddington, took a quantum leap as Boyd took the business literally out of his back yard to Wall Street and a listing on the NASDAQ exchange. Some of this impetus was fueled by a lil' ol' band from Texas. ZZ Top, led by the bearded Billy F. Gibbons, put hot rods, specifically, the Eliminator Coupe, on MTV, exposing the sport to millions of new viewers. Monster trucks, street machines, you name it, everything took a giant leap forward. In fact, we were seeing a full-circle revival of every aspect of rodding, from primered rods and chopped customs to nostalgia diggers to classic muscle cars. In short, we had it all. It was, after all, the affluent 1980s.

The 1980s saw three men take the editor's chair, Leonard Emanuelson, Pat Ganahl and finally Jeff Smith. Though confirmed enthusiasts, each was very different in his approach in steering *Hot Rod* toward its 40th anniversary in 1988. Of the three editors, Pat was perhaps the most controversial. For example, he built an 11-second Cadillac by chain-sawing away excess weight, until he was down to a frame, which looked not unlike an early dragster. He also introduced the concept of a swimsuit issue, which, while controversial at the time, remained an annual fixture on the *Hot Rod* editorial calendar.

JANUARY 1980

Make no mistake, Nomads are B-A-D! And in the January 1980 issue, HRM showed just how bad and, just how rare—less than 24,000 built in each of the three classic years: 1955, 1956, and 1957. Featured on the cover, Jim Martin's chopped 1956 Low Roller, was about as bad as it gets. Only the top and lower quarter panels were steel; everything else down to the seven-pound tailgate was either fiberglass or aluminum. The motor, a L88 fat-block, Jim built himself using L88 cylinder heads, Chevy crank and rods, J&E pistons and Speed Pro rings. Weighing just 2,600 pounds, Big Jim's 50-inch-tall wagon covered the OCIR quarter in 9.90 seconds, clocking 135+ miles per hour.

MARCH 1980
Under the masthead "Up On Two Wheels," HRM always found space to cover the two-wheeled aspect of the hot rod sport. For many years, Harley-Davidson dominated the top fuel drag bike scene, but by 1980 Japanese bikes ruled the asphalt. At the time, the world's quickest scooter was the Teson and Bernard XS1100-based Yamaha with a blistering 7.54 seconds. In comparison, the world's fastest was Vance and Hines GS1000-based Suzuki, which tripped the clocks at 199.55 miles per hour. Both bikes were Magnuson blown and both, ironically, were tuned by RC Engineering.

APRIL 1980
Two words, bracket and shoebox, entered the *Hot Rod* lexicon to describe cars like Don Barton's pro gas racer. Owned and raced by Don since 1970, his original $300 purchase saw plenty of investment in time, money and experience. The result was a 2,800-pounder powered by .060-inch-over 454 big-block with a Weiand tunnel-ram and a pair of Holley center squirters. A B&M Turbo 400 and a Dana rear completed the hardware combination. *Clownin' Around* won the 1979 Bracket Championship Award for Best Appearing car.

MAY 1980

For some reason, it didn't make the cover, but this incredible Bob D'Olivo shot of Don Garlits (Big Daddy) burning out *the Swamp Rat XXII* on the deck of the Navy's U.S.S. *Ranger* aircraft carrier is just awesome. You can imagine Bob saying, "Just one more pass, Big Daddy!" Sadly, for Garlits, this new car failed to even qualify at the preceding NHRA Winternationals and Don had to rework the chassis to remove some of its rigidity. However, within the month, the same car hit 5.79 seconds at nearly 250 miles per hour, and the Old Man was off and running in his bid to become the first triple-crown world champion (AHRA, IHRA, NHRA) in drag racing history.

DECEMBER 1980

When it comes to massive doses of drag racing, no race compares with NHRA's U.S. Nationals, held every Labor Day in Indianapolis, Indiana. The 26th running of the event was in 1980, and it lasted a full week, thanks to rain-delayed final rounds. However, the track was great and the times were great—like Marvin Graham's 5.68 in Top Fuel and Raymond Beadle's 5.96 in Funny Car. Perennial Pro Stock driver Bob Glidden, low qualifier, also turned in some stellar performances, although a red light in the final round gave the win to Lee Shepard.

FEBRUARY 1981

Designed by Harry Bradley and originally built by Lil' John Buttera, what became known as John Corno's roadster was completely reconceived in 1979 for the 1980 Oakland Roadster Show. John, of Portland, Oregon, had Mike McKennett's Restorations and Reproductions rework a pair of 1932 rails, add Porsche Red paint and detail the 1970-type thin-wall 302-inch Ford V-8. Here, in the studio, atop the elegant Bradley-designed display, you can see the car in perfect condition, as it was when it picked up the 1980 AMBR Award.

FEBRUARY 1981

Pretty in pink, Shirley Muldowney, subject of the movie *Heart Like A Wheel*, claimed her second NHRA World Championship, something no other driver in the history of national Hot Rod Association Top Fuel racing has ever accomplished at that time. The dramatic World Championship challenge came down to the final race of the NHRA campaign—the World Finals at Ontario Motor Speedway in Ontario, California. Coming into the contest, Muldowney held third place behind formed World Champion Gary Beck and Jeb Allen. Allen failed to make the field, then Muldowney put away Graham leaving Beck as her only competition. The second round found Beck a loser and Muldowney easily put away Frank Bradley to take the trophy.

JULY 1981
At the Grand National Roadster Show in Oakland in January of 1981, Boyd Coddington debuted the Vern Luce Coupe and to say that it knocked the rodding fraternity on its collective butt would be an understatement. Certainly they should have been prepared by the smooth rods emanating from the milling machine of Lil' John Buttera, but the coupe that graced the cover of the July 1981 issue was in a league of its own. Designed by Thom Taylor and crafted by the team of Boyd, Buttera, Steve Davis, Dan Fink, Terry Hegman, Vic Kitchens, Art Chrisman and others, the car set the style for the next decade and a half. The car in the background was 20-year-old Marty Camp's 1971 Z28 Camaro.

AUGUST 1981

Drag racing was born out of illegal hot rod racing on the streets, and in 1981 the sport came full circle—kinda—with the First Annual Hot Rod Drags. Held at Fremont Drag Strip, Fremont, California, it was definitely a run-what-ya-brung event, as evidenced by this shot of Pete Chapouris (The California Kid) facing off Tommy Ivo (TV). Ivo, it transpired, had more than horsepower to his advantage and completely psyched out The Kid when he told him, "Pull way over the right when I come by, or the blast will blow you away." Well, Pete was so busy anticipating the shock wave he missed a shift and, despite a seven-second lead, lost the race.

OCTOBER 1981

When it was introduced, few would have believed that the venerable VW Beetle would become grist for the hot rodder's mill, but with the advent of "Cal Look" a whole new breed of cool was born. Slammed, louvered, flamed, rodded and even chopped, Cal Look VWs hit the scene hard with dedicated events, even drag races, which continue to this day. On the left it was Craig Nuss of Arcadia, California, in his 1969, and on the right it was Don Fontaine, also of Arcadia, with his full-race street car complete with wheelie bars.

NOVEMBER 1981

"Will they become the 1957 Chevy of the 80s?" was the question asked of the Buick Regal in the November 1981 issue. History has answered the question but there's is no doubt that for a while there, Buick had a tiger by the tail. Proving the point were two of the industry's big guns. On the left, Junior Johnson with his 1981 Regal specially prepared for Darrell Waltrip and Riverside Raceway. Incidentally, at that time, Buick had won 17 of 21 NASCAR races. To Junior's right was Gale Banks with his all-out twin-turbo street engine prepared by Gale for use in *Hot Rod*'s 1981 Regal project car, immediately behind him.

'82

FEBRUARY 1982
Ever the innovator, Lil' John Buttera blew 'em away again with his version of Henry's answer to the Model T. Stripped of all nonessentials, his stretched, smoothed and silvered bullet featured a Gale Banks twin-turbo Buick V-6 package, B&M Turbo 400 trans, Lil' John fabricated front end painted black and more than 5,500 on the speedo from just one cross-country trip.

JULY 1982

Something old, something new. In this case the something old was not as old as it appeared. Jamie Musselman's roadster, driven here by its creator, Boyd Coddington, was America's Most Beautiful Roadster for 1982 and the first of six wins for Boyd. Designed by Thom Taylor and masterfully executed by Boyd's team, which included John Buttera, Steve Davis, Dan Fink, Art Chrisman Terry Hegman and Vic Kitchens, the roadster set new standards in construction and new directions in design. Something blue was an Contemporary Classic Cobra. Based on the venerable AC/Shelby Cobra of the 1960s, this kit featured original-style round-tube frame and 427 inches of side-oiling Ford.

SEPTEMBER 1982

Over the years, *Hot Rod* tried to impart as much behind-the-scenes information as it could to its readers and cutaway renderings such as this example by David Kimble were staple fodder. In this case, David's subject was the work of veteran car builder Don Edmunds' Autoresearch Coil-Over Sprint Car. Owned by Joe Binter of San Diego, California, and driven by Jeff Heywood, the car sported coil-over shocks on all four corners with a variable-rate helper torsion bar for suspension tuning. Unconventional compared to most torsion-bar-only sprinters, the Edmunds sprinter eliminated about 75 pounds of weight and enjoyed better weight transfer.

NOVEMBER 1982

The hot rod sport has always been about extremes, and these two cars are prime examples. Used to illustrate a Graffiti Nights theme, they exemplified the street scene of the early-1980's. In the foreground, Allen Owen's 'Cuda was where it was at as far as candy tangerine streamlined babies went. Set up in pro stock-style with skinny center lines up front and an attack of the fats in the rear, it was powered by a 340-inch Chrysler. At the other end of the spectrum sat Pete Eastwood and Rick Barakat's prime mover. This down and dirty 32 set its own trends for cruisin' cool with brown suede body. Built in just 12 weeks from spare parts, it stopped the OCIR clocks with a 11.59 elapsed time while recording a top speed of 117.49 miles per hour.

OCTOBER 1982
One of the all-time favorite hot rods was the 1940 Willys coupe, and one of the all-time favorite Willys coupes was that of Fred Stone, Tim Woods, and Doug Cook. Campaigned aggressively in the gasser wars of the 1960s, the Stone, Woods and Cook Willys was raced from 1961 when, on its first outing, it broke both ends of the national B/GS record at Lions Drag Strip, until its retirement in 1966. One of the biggest crowd pleasers of all time, it was also one of the first whose owners capitalized on that fact through clever promotion. Known as the *Swinderl A*, this is the very same car that was racing in 1966 and it sports the very same slicks. Back then it ran consistent midnines at close to 160 miles per hour.

'83

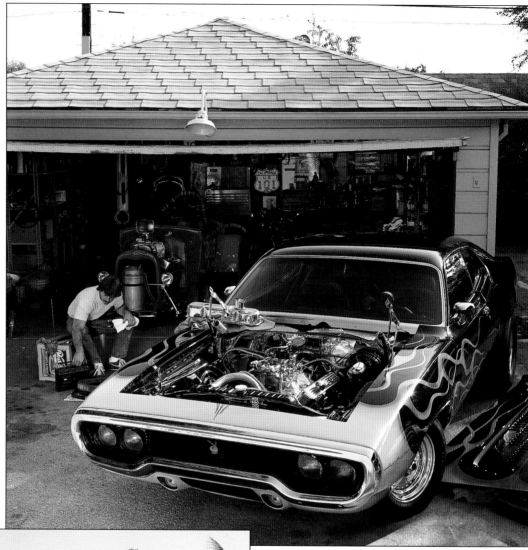

FEBRUARY 1983

The theme of the February 1983 issue was Street Heros and for the cover HRM borrowed the driveway of Pete Eastwood (P-Wood), where Pat Broiler photographed 23-year-old Mike Mattern's 1971 Plymouth Satellite in the style of a Norman Rockwell painting. Mike, from Chula Vista, California, bought the car from his mom and spent two years emulating the nose-down NASCAR look. With 440-inch six-pack power, mom's grocery getter netted double coupons and a quarter-mile in 13.78 seconds at 101.23 miles per hour. Sitting behind Mike is Tony Piner's 233-mile per hour A-bodied salt shaker.

MAY 1983

Linda Vaughn, the first lady of motorsports and front lady for Hurst products, proudly displays Warren Johnson's new Hurst Olds Pro Stocker. When Oldsmobile decided to re-enter the arena, it did it in style, and when Dick Chrysler acquired Hurst, he was determined to thrust the company back into the limelight. The marriage was a natural. Meanwhile, Warren Johnson teamed up with Olds Division to redesign the venerable rat motor and fix all of its inherent problems. The result was a killer engine. For example, by using different stroke lengths, the block capacity could be increased from 350 to 650 inches. Warren expected mid-sevens and speeds above 180 miles per hour.

JUNE 1983

Hot rodding has always been a father-and-son sport, evidenced in the June 1983 issue, when the cover sported the beard-and-no-beard duos of Chuck and Chuckie Lombardo and Jim and Chester McNamara in the foreground. The 1957 Chevy way in the back was a $500 basket case when 13-year-old Chuckie began a four-year project that would leave him $4,500 lighter in the pocket. His father's brandywine roadster featured a Wescott fiberglass Deuce body powered by a Keith Black 4-71 blown 350 Chevy—it went on to win the America's Most beautiful Roadster Award at the 1983 Oakland Roadster Show. Chester McNamara's 1957 Bell Air two-door employed a fully balanced and blueprinted 327. His dad's full-fendered, Weber-carbed Deuce roadster was built at Lombardo's California Street Rods.

SEPTEMBER 1983
Undoubtedly, no other car in the history of the sport has had more impact on he general public than Billy F. Gibbons' Top Eliminator coupe, *ZZ*. However, when it was photographed here, outside Rae's in Santa Monica, California, by Randy Lorentzen, it was not yet the international icon it became. Built primarily by Don Thelen, the swoopy 1933 Ford displayed Kenny Youngblood-designed *ZZ* graphics, and went on to expose hot rodding to millions in the MTV generation. The other cars were Shane DeWitt's 1957 Chevy three-door and Ted Ozbirn's 1970 GTO, *Judge*.

DECEMBER 1983
Since its introduction, the 1955 Chevy has always been a *Hot Rod* favorite. For the December 1983 issue, the staff gathered around Lee Fabry's low down, mean and nasty, black and flamed, chopped double-nickel. Painted by Devan Noonan of Final Touch, the car was powered by a 1971 350-inch Chevy.

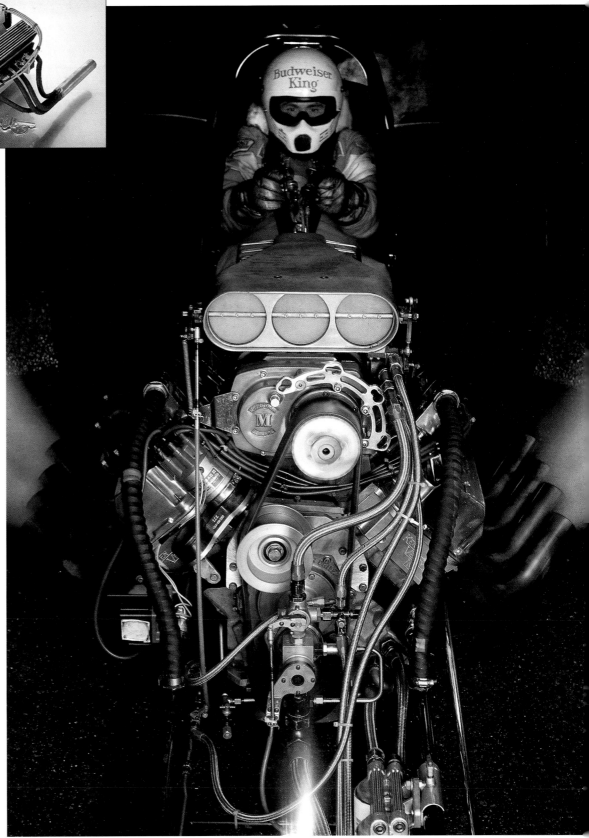

'84

MARCH 1984

Sometimes, great things do come in small packages. The antithesis of hot rodding's credo, "There's no substitute for cubic inches," was evidenced in Gary Conley's quarter-scale V-8. Based on the small-block Chevy, the world's smallest, running production engines were just 5 inches long, 4-1/2 inches wide and 6 inches tall. Running on model airplane fuel with 20 percent oil and 10-20 percent nitro, they had a capacity of 1.53 cubic inches (28 cc), weighed in at six pounds and put out 1-1/2 horsepower. Operating in the 2,000–9,500-rpm range, they featured a square bore and stroke of 5/8 of an inch. In 1984, he was selling them for $1,700 each.

MARCH 1984

At the other end of the spectrum from Gary Conley's diminutive motor was Kenny Berstein's new Budweiser King Funny Car. At the time, Kevin Boales said it was a story of staggering numbers: "A good running funny car goes 0-60 in about a second; it will accomplish that in 50 feet. The drivers are subjected to about 4g, and the car would drain a typical Ford gas tank in less than a minute." Each quarter-mile blast cost more than $2,500. What was really interesting though, was the discovery that nitro engines could get by without an ignition system, once they were making power. Kenny made a run in 1983 when the mag was not operating after the launch, because the drive gear pin had sheared. No one noticed, and the car still ran a 6 flat!

MAY 1984

The NHRA's season opener, the Winternationals held annually in Pomona, California, can generally be guaranteed to produce some exciting racing, and 1984 was no exception. Titled "The Comeback Nationals" by Leonard Emanuelson, the event saw the return of many veterans like Don Garlits, Judy Lilly, and Ken Dondero. One man who had a particularly exciting ride was Mert Littlefield, when his Dodge Daytona-bodied funny car got loose in the mid-range and kissed the guard rail. The impact tore the right front wheel off the car, which allowed the front end, including the fuel tank, to come in contact with the pavement. There was so much fire, Mert lost vision and hit the guardrail again. Thanks to all the safety features in place even then, Mert suffered no burns or bruises.

APRIL 1984

Of all the monster trucks ever built, Bob Chandler's *Bigfoot* was the first and probably the most popular. *Bigfoot III* was then the latest in a nine-year parade emanating from Chandler's Hazelwood, Missouri, home. The first, built to promote the products Bob sold in his Midwest Four-Wheel Drive Center, appeared in a movie called *Take this Job and Shove It*, and the rest, as they say, is history. *Bigfoot III* was powered by a Ford Motorsport Arias-Root 460-inch Boss 429 block with a Hampton 6-71 on top. Making about 600 horsepower, it rode on two five-ton military truck front axles and 66-inch Goodyear Terra tires.

DECEMBER 1984

For the last issue of 1984, *Hot Rod* produced "A Guide to the Wild World of Street Rodding." To illustrate the theme, Don Kleine of El Cajon, California, provided the cover car. Based on a 1931 Model A that had originally been rodded in the 1950s, Don took the 1980s theme of more must be better and added his own statement, in the form of a 6-71 blown Chrysler Hemi.

'85

JANUARY 1985

Barry Wiggins captured the extremes of the on-going interest in hot rod trucks. The diminutive (only in comparison) screamin' yellow 1928 Model A was the ride of choice for Orvel Lynes from Colton, California. A Holley-equipped Buick V-6 resided behind the Deuce grille and under the three-piece hood. At the other, or, perhaps upper, extreme was *Bear Foot*. A truck of monster proportions, *Bear Foot* was built by Jack Willman and Fred Shafer of Madison, Illinois. Powered by a 800-horsepower 6-71 blown ZL-1 454 Chevy, *Bear Foot* rode on a pair of five-ton "top load" Rockwell axles.

FEBRUARY 1985

In the top three of the baby boomer list of most memorable hot rods, there is surely a place for Kookie's T-bucket, which appeared in the TV show *77 Sunset Strip*, along with Pete Chapouris' *The California Kid* and Billy F. Gibbons *Eliminator*. Originally built by Norm Grabowski, the Kookie car inspired many to emulate the look. One such enthusiast was Jack Dooney who said at the time, "I was not trying to copy Norm's T, but rather duplicate the 'look' Norm achieved." A mixture of old and "newstalgia," the Jack-attack screams out for attention.

APRIL 1985

It took three Petersen Publishing photographers, Bob D'Olivo, Jim Brown, and Pat Broiler, to capture this high-tech shot of a high-tech race car. Developed by Triad Services, Warren, Michigan, for Mr. Gasket, it was intended that the cars' chassis would be sold as a kit. What made it unusual was that the tube ends, rather than being "fish mouthed," were designed as castings to allow the use of tubing cut squarely on the ends. According to Mr. Gasket, kits for the Gasket Grand Sport 'Vette would include prebent tubing and fittings or, buyers could select from a variety of fittings packaged individually. Mr. Corvette, Zora Arkus Duntov, was retained by Mr. Gasket to help think up new uses for the casting technique.

144

JULY 1985

The Fat attack came in the form of Pete Chapouris', of Pete and Jake's Hot Rod Parts, 1939 convertible. Built in honor of his father, who owned a rodded 1939 when they were new, Pete's purple plumpness galvanized a trend encouraging rodders to step out of the box and explore canvases other than early Fords. In the background, between Jake on the left and Pete, Jack Robinson (Fat Jack) squeezed his own effort. Unfortunately, after Jack sold the Orange Crush to George Striegel, it was destroyed in a dramatic rolling wreck at Baylands Raceway Park, where driver Dave Condit reportedly put parts of the car through the lights in 9.17 seconds.

AUGUST 1985

Under the catch-all subtitle "Street Racing—The Culture That Will Not Die," the August 1985 issue looked long and hard at those who liked to motivate straight—legal and illegal. One of those who liked to do it legal was Gerry Steiner, seen here smokin' the full quarter at Brian Burnett and Tom Prufer's Fifth Annual Nostalgia Nationals. Behind the wheel of the alky-burning, legendary Mooneyham & Sharp 1934, Gerry boiled those ol' M&H hides until there was no smoke left in 'em.

DECEMBER 1985

Legendary drag racer Joe Amato was the first top fuel driver to take his car over 260 miles per hour. The question asked in the December 1985 issue was, "Will it be the first over 270?" The car, depicted here by illustrator John Batchelor, consisted of a Swindahl Chassis Components 260-inch frame and a Tim Richards-built Keith Black motor, which was actually pretty straightforward without exotic dual-pump fuel system or computer-aided tuning. Instead, Richards relied on precise Super Stock-style engine prep and a common-sense approach to car setup. However, one of the contributory factors in the 260-mile per hour run was the Eldon Rasmussen-designed "high-wing," which produced the same downforce as more common wings but with less drag.

JANUARY 1986

While the January 1986 issue looked at new ways to boost performance, this Gary Stiles shot of Willy Borsch (Wild Willy) at Pomona in 1968 showed the tried and true method, which says there is no substitute for cubic inches. Included in a Gray Baskerville article entitled "Fuel Altereds Forever," and with the tag line, "Forget all that Other Stuff, These are the Real Hot Rods," Gray couldn't have been more right on. These real hot rods were governed by engine setback (generally 25 percent of the wheelbase), body shape (strictly prewar in configuration), and driver placement (in front of the third member). Wild Willy himself best summed up the class when he described them as, "Nothin' more than T-buckets with top fuel motors in them."

SEPTEMBER 1986

By the mid-1980s, nostalgia had a strangle hold on the world and no where more so than in the hobby of hot rodding. All over the country, enthusiasts were scouring barns and garages for old race cars and snapping them up before the prices went through the roof. As with all things, those with a pedigree, are worth more than others. One such race car was this seriously chopped Model-A coupe of Art and Lloyd Chrisman. It had been over 30 years since the Chrismans had thundered their incomparable coupe over Bonneville's 40 million-year-old salt, using a freebie body and a pair of welded together 1940 Ford hoods to form the envelope. The coupe was eventually sold to George Barris, who fixed it up Hollywood style for the *Dobie Gillis* TV show. However, Bob Larivee purchased the car and had Art restore it to its bronze brilliance.

OCTOBER 1986

Indianapolis, Indiana, was, in 1986, home to three of the nation's most prestigious motorsports events: The Indy 500, the NHRA U.S. Nationals drags and the *Hot Rod* Super Nationals. While the first two require a large chunk of change to participate, the *Hot Rod* Super Nationals was an event for everybody who had the price of admission and a clean street car. And, what made it special was that even without the multimillion dollar investment, entrants still got the chance to circumnavigate the Indianapolis Motor Speedway—albeit for a brief two-hour period. It was an opportunity few participants will ever forget.

NOVEMBER 1986

Since its inception, Pike's Peak has always attracted an eclectic bunch of racers. It has also been viewed by manufacturers as a perfect venue to test their mettle and promote their wares. On July 12, 1986, more than 10,000 spectators were astounded when the most spectacular drive up the hill was turned in by three-time Indy 500 winner Bobby Unser, Sr., driving a 1986 four-wheel-drive Audi Sport Quattro. Shattering Michelle Mouton's previous course record by some 16 seconds, Unser covered the course in 11:09:22 and forever changed the face of racing to the clouds.

DECEMBER 1986
Photographed by Pat Ganahl for the cover of the December 1986 issue, Dave Mordhorst's 1955 Chevy evidenced all of the contemporary trends including monochromatic paint, big blower and in-da-dirt stance. It was the perfect image for an issue that included not only the Top 10 of 1986, of which Dave's car was one, but also *Hot Rod*'s 10 Best Hot Rods ever. Featured in the January 1986 issue, Dave's 6-71 blown 409 was built almost entirely by Dave and his uncle Milo in a one-car garage in Carson City, Nevada.

AUGUST 1987

Over the years, the name Jerry Moreland has appeared in the pages of *Hot Rod* on numerous occasions and always connected with a significant piece of machinery. For example, the August 1987 issue featured this 1957 Chevy, which could well be the factory's single remaining quasi-production race car. Originally sold in Gardena, California, it's quite possible this car was raced on southern California tracks like nearby Saugus. Original cars featured a strengthened frame, fuel-injected motor and reinforced suspension. Known as Black Widows, the first to appear in *Hot Rod* in the September 1957 issue was photographed by Ray Brock at Pike's Peak. Brock wrote, "The only fuel-injected 1957 Chevy to show up for the race was well driven by Bob Korf, last year's runner-up for the climb, but couldn't keep up with the blown Fords."

OCTOBER 1987

The resurrection of early race cars for nostalgia-type racing became a craze in the 1980s and one of the *Hot Rod* editors got a tip that an early blown-Chrysler-powered dragster was languishing in someone's back yard. The tip was left uninvestigated for two years, but upon a whim the lead was traced and, sure enough, under the rotting cover sat a complete top gas dragster that hadn't turned a wheel in anger for more than 20 years. Complete with a front-mounted Potvin blower, the rail had a Chassis Research frame, Halibrand rear wheels with hand-lettered M&H Racemasters and candy red paint.

NOVEMBER 1987
In an issue crammed full of summer action, the November 1987 edition contained a build-up article on the construction of the B&M/PAW motor for Pete Chapouris' *Limefire* roadster. Pete's plan was to build a hot rod that he could drive to the drags, run 10-second quarters and drive home. The PAW combo included a four-bolt 350 block bored .030 over and fitted with a 400 crank for a total displacement of 383 cubic inches. Weighing in at 2,200 pounds and with 495 horsepower, the roadster eventually ran a best of 10.75.

JULY 1988

The trend for mini trucks was hot n' heavy in the late 1980s. *Hot Rod* described it as, "A Splashy New Craze," which was perfectly described by this dancing bed flipping Robert Ramirez into the pool. The truck was owned and operated (remote control), by Dee Massei of Cupertino, California. Dee bought a base model 1987 Mazda B2200, then had Heinrich apply candy apple graphics over the stock paint. She then lowered it to the max, fitted a 500-watt Kenwood stereo and had a triple-ram hydraulic bed installed—that's *Hot Rod*'s kinda gal.

MAY 1988

The staff of *Hot Rod* magazine have always been enthusiasts first, journalists second and Gray Baskerville (Yer Ol' Dad) is no different. He still drives a Deuce roadster, but in the 1960s he and his friend, Paul Horning, decided to go racing. From an assortment of spare parts and with a great deal of help from Ernie Murashige's M&V Automotive, they built the *Rollin' Rice Bowl*. It debuted as a B/Altered the week after the 1963 Winternationals, was never beaten in class, and capped off its short career with a class win (over 32 B/As) at the 1963 Indy Nats. Gray always had a place in his heart for the car, and in 1986 a bunch of his friends including Pete and Jake, Pete Eastwood, John Buttera, Boyd Coddington, Art Chrisman, Jim Davis, Andy and Roy Brizio, Gene Adams, and many more pitched in to build a replica without Gray knowing it. The car was presented to him by Tom Medley at Fremont.

154

AUGUST 1988

The cover blurb said, "7-sec. Shoeboxes" and it wasn't lying. As controversial as they may have been, and they were called "outlaws" by some sanctioning bodies, but they wowed the crowds with their nostalgic styling and futuristic performance. As Gray told it, "You ain't seen nothin' till you've had the gut-grabbing pleasure of watching a 7/8-scale 1957 Chevy rocking the 1,320 in seven seconds flat at over 199 miles per hour." In this case it was Jim Bryant's *Thunder Craft* that he was talking about. With Rob Vandergriff behind the wheel, it was, at the time, the fastest brick in the country. Power came from an Eagle Race Engine-prepared rat Chevy and lots of NOS.

OCTOBER 1988

The subject of one of *Hot Rod*'s first fold-out centerfolds, in the October 1988 issue, was this immaculate, almost toy-like 1933 Willys. Built for Joe Hrudka, then of Mr. Gasket fame, by Lil' John Buttera, the car exploited all the milling machine talents John had amassed over the years. John envisioned a Mercedes-like hot rod with clean, simple understated lines. The original 1933 body was massaged by Steve Davis, Tiki Alvarez and Terry Hegman, who installed the VW headlights. Buttera built most of the rest, including the complete billet aluminum front and rear independent suspension systems and those wheels which he whittled out of four large hunks of billet aluminum. He knew he could do it but John kept putting the job off for three years because even though they look the same, all four wheels are different, being big and small, left and right.

DECEMBER 1988

In the year of a new T-Bird from Ford, some like Matt and Debbie Hay were just finishing off modified versions of the previous car. That's not to take anything away from their incredible effort. Their twice-blown 'Bird rode on an Alston chassis, which was altered to radically lower the car. For power, Matt turned to Alan Root, who devised a 351-inch Windsor that would be capable of putting the 'Bird through the traps in double-quick time while still being streetable. Boost was provided to two B&M blowers mounted side-by-side ahead of the motor. A pair of Mikuni 44-millimeter carbs fed fuel to the blowers, while copious amounts of nitrous oxide were pumped into the B&M manifold. It was worth the effort, as Matt and Debbie picked up the Street Machine Nationals Pro Street Award in DuQuoin, Illinois.

JANUARY 1989

"Tomorrow's Hot Rodding Today" was the cover blurb for the January 1989 issue, which introduced the Pontiac Banshee concept car. As is often the case, the reality of the production Firebird did not quite match up to the dream car, which sported very swoopy styling and a 230-horsepower, 4.0-liter aluminum V-8. Sadly, the one-piece block and cylinder head design was left over from the GM Manhattan project and did not see production. Nevertheless, Banshee rode on a custom tube frame designed to incorporate then-current Corvette independent suspension, and the motor drove the rear wheels in conventional F-body style.

MAY 1989
At times, hot rods veered from their true lineage and became street rods, but the late 1980s saw a definite return to the roots. Boyce Asquith's thundering yellow screamer definitely put the hot back in rod. Boyce, a chrome plater from Pomona, California, powered his statement with a 495-inch Bow-Tie Chevy with a B&M blower and B&M drive train including a B&M Turbo 400. With 900 horses pulling the carriage, the car almost broke into the eights, running regularly in the low nines. It was case of Asquith, and ye shall receive.

MAY 1989
The bad-ass shoebox craze was in full kill toward the end of the decade, with Pro boys using all kinds of odd-bods as the basis for their race cars. While it was some years after the release of the namesake book and movie, Richard Earle's 3/4-scale carbon-fiber 1958 Plymouth Fury, *Christine,* regularly tripped the lights in the midseven-second region at 190-plus miles per hour. A Funny Car-style tube frame was home to the Dave Koffel-built 557-inch Wedge motor—a mighty Mopar based on a Keith Black aluminum block with B-1 heads and one of Mike Norica's two-stage ICE nitrous systems.

AUGUST 1989

In keeping with *Hot Rod*'s tradition of covering all aspect of the exciting world of motorsports, the August 1989 issue featured this great racing action shot by Jon Asher during the Trans-Am race at Long Beach. The start, as you can see, was wild with a few too many cars trying to fill too little space. Deborah Gregg (right) didn't even make it to the first corner after her Camaro smashed into the back of Kenny Hendrick's, resulting in a three-car pile up involving Rick Ware's 'Vette, Jerry Kuhn's Camaro and Mike Ciasulli's Oldsmobile.

The NINETIES

APRIL 1993
Old hot rods never die. So that saying goes and in many cases that's true. It's certainly true in the case of the famous 2D car. Featured first on the cover and inside the April 1950 issue of *Hot Rod*, the car was built by Bob and Bill Pierson and by the end of 1949 the *Pierson Bros. Coupe*, as it was and is known, was the fastest closed car in hot rodding's short history. Actively raced until the early 1990s, the car was eventually purchased by Bruce Meyer and restored by Pete Chapouris' SO-CAL Speed Shop.

Chapter 5

Today and Tomorrow

Mature! Fifty years old. Who'd have thought it possible? Certainly not Robert E. Petersen, when he and his hot rodding buddy Bob Lindsay, decided to launch *Hot Rod* in January 1948. Now, more than 600 issues later, with *Hot Rod* the flagship publication of Petersen Publishing, a public company traded on the NASDAQ Exchange, *Hot Rod* looks forward to the next 50.

In the ensuing years, the sport has withstood assault from every quarter, including oil shortages, government regulation and environmental issues. Nevertheless, hot rodders have shown that they are just as environmentally conscious as the rest of the population and no matter what the various regulatory agencies have thrown at the hobbyist, the industry has always come back to prove that it can build 'em clean and green. And *Hot Rod*, with its various high-profile project vehicles, has always been there carrying the torch, leading the way with hard-hitting, cutting-edge technical articles that help the enthusiast continue to enjoy his hobby.

While *Hot Rod* continues to look forward to a future stronger than ever with unprecedented growth in all aspects of motorsports, there's also an equally strong return to the roots and, at the root of it all was *Hot Rod* magazine. Whether it was Bob Petersen standing out on the dry lakes one dusty day with his trusty Speed Graphic camera, or Jeff Koch mixing it up with the caviar crowd at the Pebble Beach Historic Concours d'Elegance, *Hot Rod* is there.

In the driver's seat is Ro McGonegal, whose job it is to steer this blown and injected, high-horsepower, but these days computer-controlled, ship into the next millennium. The 50th anniversary issue, January 1998, with a Chip Foose-penned, Roy Brizio-built recreation of the first-ever *Hot Rod* cover car, boasts "Our Biggest Issue Ever," and with 228 pages, it is undoubtedly a mere prelude to what is to come.

FEBRUARY 1990
Gray Baskerville ushered in a new era in the February 1990 issue when he opined that, "The reason most hot rodders can't build low-buck rods is that they're afraid to use their imaginations. It's easier to throw money at chrome-plating a Camaro than to opt for a sow's rear and turn it into a silk purse." To illustrate his low-buck options, Gray chose these four new-wave street machines that evidenced ingenuity and imagination. In the back it was Scott Montegerard's 1976 Grand Prix, and from left to right it was Mike Rinaldi's *Hugger Orange* 1967 Pontiac LeMans with 454 power, Daniel Winiecki's 1969 Torino with 428 Cobra power, and David Jelinek's 1976 Laguna, which was powered by a B&M-blown 355-inch mouse.

JULY 1990 Prompted by some suggestion from designer Thom Taylor, *Hot Rod* magazine began a campaign encouraging its readers to "Dare to be Different," and boy did they ever respond! Cars that only had ever been ridiculed and would never have been considered legitimate hot rod fodder suddenly came under the hammer. Take, for example, John DePorter's Scottsdale, Arizona-based *Bad Cad*. Stuffed with a 526-inch, Mooneyham 8-71-blown all-aluminum Rodeck, this 1959 Cadillac Coupe De Ville ran in the Top Sportsman class.

MARCH 1990
Back in 1986, Gary Gillette contacted Marcel de Lay at Custom Metal Shaping about reworking his original 1932 Ford. The list of modifications that Gary desired prompted Marcel to suggest that for the price of all these changes he could probably build a complete new body to Gary's specifications. While a chassis was prepared at California Street Rods, Marcel and his two sons, Marc and Luc, began work and in just six weeks they had hammered and shaped the first all-new Deuce three-window in more than 50 years. And, it's a body so well executed that only a trained eye can spot the subtle differences from an original. It also started a trend toward brand new sheet metal.

▲ SEPTEMBER 1990

In the summer of 1990, a couple of *Hot Rod* staffers, Steve Anderson and Rob Kinnan, had the opportunity for the road trip of a life-time. The two were to drive *CadZZilla* cross country to Canfield, Ohio, for the *Hot Rod* Super Nationals. Sandstorms and rain did not deter the drivers who covered more than 2,200 miles in one of the nation's most famous hot rods.

AUGUST 1990

The introduction on the 1988 line of Chevy and GMC full-size trucks spawned a whole new genre of hot rods—sport trucks. Previously, trucks had been utilitarian but with new, car-like interiors and a Chevy small-block driving the rear wheels, they became the modern-day sports car. Leading the pack with his inspirational ideas was designer Thom Taylor, whose GMC fleetside in the August 1990 issue set the style for the next decade. It featured Bell tech lowering, Boyd's wheels, paint by Pete Santini, and striping by Steve Stanford.

APRIL 1991

America's sports car, the Corvette, has by nature always been prime meat for the hot rodder's cleaver, and *Hot Rod*'s 1991 swimsuit issue featured three excellent early examples. Bringing up the rear was Steve Roth's 283-powered Pro Street-style 1962. Making a graphic statement to the front left was Tom Vinciguerra's 1961 model, fitted with a potent 355-cubic inch small-block backed up by a four-speed Muncie. On the far right it was Rod Saboury's flea market acquisition 1959 that became a show stopper after only 60 days. Tubbed for big tires, Rod made it equally powerful by fitting a 6-71 blown 350.

JANUARY 1991

For 30 years, Cliff Hansem dreamt of this car. In that time, he enjoyed a long career of racing Formula 3, Formula 2, and group C2 prototypes around the globe. In 1990, thanks to Roy Brizio, he got to drive his life-long dream car. Roy chopped an original 1933 Ford 3 inches before channeling the body another 3 inches over the rails, which were a combination of 191934 Ford fronts and 1932 Ford rears. For propulsion, he chose a Bruno Gianoli-built 331 Hemi, which deceptively has a Holley 3310 four-barrel beneath the injector hat, which sits on top of a BDS housing and intake. Incidentally, smokin' 'em in the background of this Steve Anderson shot was the Jim and Mike McClennan Champion Speed Shop AA/Fuel Dragster at Sears Point Raceway.

JULY 1991

In a very short time, Pro Modified racing became a highly competitive, professional drag racing class populated with some of the fastest, most radically streamlined and customized doorslammers this side of Bonneville. Classic hot rodding body styles and modifications such as chopping, channeling, and sectioning became commonplace, and Robbie Vandergriff was considered to have one of the most radical and streamlined bodies in the class when his 1957 first appeared in 1988. However, by 1991, it was grossly outdated, so Robbie decided to build this new car. The body, built by Randy Headrick of Aerostar Fiberglass, was placed atop a Jerry Haas chassis and fitted with a 632-inch nitrous sucking Chevy built by Mike Hedgecock of Eagle Racing engines. The motor made 1,215 horsepower sans nitrous.

AUGUST 1991

When, among other desirable automobiles, you have in your stable *Eliminator* coupe and *CadZZilla*, it's hard to know what to do next. However, a chance airport encounter between Willie G. Davidson and Billy F. Gibbons of ZZ Top resulted in not one, but two additions to the ZZilla garage. Designed to complement the Caddy, the pair of Fat Boy-based *HogZZillas* were assembled by Pete Chapouris and Bob Bauder with help form the usual suspects, including Steve Davis, Tiki Alvarez, Tim Beard, John Carambia and Jim Jacobs. Built in just 58 days, the bikes led the annual 26,000-strong parade around Daytona's tri-oval.

MARCH 1992

While it graced the cover of the December 1991 issue, *Hot Rod*'s clean *Green Machine* 1955 Chevy was wrapped up in the March 1992 issue. Built to prove to skeptical government agencies that the aftermarket had the capabilities of cleaning up older cars rather than scrapping, the *Green Machine* drove away from the 1991 Specialty Equipment Market Association (SEMA) Show with the Overall Star of the Show Award. The *Green Machine* received the because it best represented the spirit of the SEMA Show and complying with 1979 Camaro emissions standards, demonstrated the innovative use of legal aftermarket products.

JULY 1992

A small step for man, a giant step for street hot rodding. Designed by Larry Erickson and built at Hot Rods by Boyd, the Aluma Coupe was controversial not only for its design but also for its choice of powerplant. Powered by an RC Engineering-tuned, turbocharged Mitsubishi four banger, the *Cosmic Coupe*, as *Hot Rod* called it, drew derision from purists who thought any hot rod as American as apple pie should have an American V-8 for motive force. No matter what your camp, there's no denying that the Aluma Coupe stretched the envelope of hot rod design, generated great press for sponsor Mitsubishi and took hot rod design on a whole new trajectory.

NOVEMBER 1992

The late Jim Ewing had a dream, and that was to build a road car that he could drive to Bonneville, run 200 miles per hour, and then drive home. Eventually, Jim found a $700 1953 Lowey post coupe, which he painted salt-flat purple, complete with flying eyeball, and powered with a humongous, all-aluminum 690-inch, 820-horse Donovan/Olds motor. In 1991, Jim took his passion to the salt and clocked a respectable 226 miles per hour through the mufflers.

AUGUST 1992

New kids on the block, torch bearers if you like, are something that graying rod fathers have been looking for to continue the sport in their image. One bright spark on an otherwise dark horizon was a 22-year-old Troy Trepanier of Manteno, Illinois. Troy, who sneaked into the limelight on the *Hot Rod* Magazine Victory Tour West in 1990 with his *Greenhouse Effect* 1960 Impala, made a return appearance with this 1950 Buick Sedanette. Found rusting away outside and autoparts store, Troy turned the Buford into a Bumongous happening of giant proportions. Subtle body mods, painted-out chrome and 510 inches of nitrated rat pack powered Troy to the cover of the August 1992 issue.

SEPTEMBER 1992

In 1992, *Hot Rod* went in search of the 10 fastest street cars in America. Actually, the 10 quickest, but according to story author Joe Pettitt, "fastest sounded better." When the smoke cleared, there sat Mac Carter on top of the heap. Max's 1966 Nova blistered the asphalt in just 8.454 seconds, with a speed of 157 miles per hour, due in no small part to 557 inches of Crane roller-cammed Bow-Tie block capped with aluminum Bow-Tie heads, a Sonny Leonard-modified Holley Pro Dominator intake and twin Barry Grant 1150 carbs. Oh. And a heavy dose of laughing gas.

JANUARY 1993

Perhaps more than any other designer, the fertile mind of Thom Taylor has pushed the envelope of hot rod and custom car design. Responsible for many of Boyd Coddington's early successes, Thom went to him in 1992 with this concept for a wildly modified 1957 Chevy. Boyd, in turn, had a canny knack of finding customers, and in this case turned to Joe Hrudka of the Mr. Gasket empire. Joe, a collector of 1957 Chevies, jumped at the chance to have his name associated with this Hot Rods by Boyd creation and *CheZoom* remains one of the quintessential customized 1957s. *CheZoom* graced the cover of the January 1993 issue.

JULY 1993

The constant search for ways to reduce the cost, go racing on the cheap and still have a heap of fun is often what makes motorsport such an interesting phenomenon. In the early 1990s, one promising answer seemed to be Dwarf Cars. With 5/8-scale, jalopy-style bodies similar to cars of the 1930s through 1940s, Dwarf Cars are powered by 1.250-cc-or-less motorcycle engines, transversely mounted to spin a driveshaft from the bike tranny. They make over 100 horsepower and run 14-second quarter-miles. Maximum dimensions were 38 inches tall and 60 wide with a 73-inch wheelbase. Many were clocked at over 100 miles per hour on big tracks.

MARCH 1993

Under the title "The Great Pretender" *Hot Rod* magazine, in March 1993, looked under the skin of a NASCAR stock car to see how stock was stock. The car in question was the Kodak-sponsored, Morgan-McClure-owned 1992 Chevy Lumina driven by Ernie Irvan (Swervin' Irvan). Although it's about as far from stock as you can get, the Lumina is still, a V-6-powered front-wheel drive sedan. Nevertheless, NASCAR "stockers" provide a unique type of racing excitement due in no small part to their 358-inch pushrod engines, which produce almost 700 horsepower at 8,000 rpm and 500-plus lb-ft of torque at 6,000 rpm for 500 miles.

SEPTEMBER 1993

Like a 1932 Ford or a 1955 Chevy, the Camaro has always provided a suitable canvas for the hot rodder's brush. In the early 1990s, the style in vogue was pro street. Tubbed until there was no trunk, only room for a fuel cell, and loaded down in the front with 468 inches of Rat power, Jim Treppa's ultrasano 1968 peeled off a 9.64-second, 135-mile per hour pass at the 1992 Fastest Street Car In American Shootout. Unfortunately, the tranny scattered at about 1,000 feet, so it was replaced with a Rick Bewick Turbo 400, along with a 565-inch Tyler Crockett motor in time for the 1993 event.

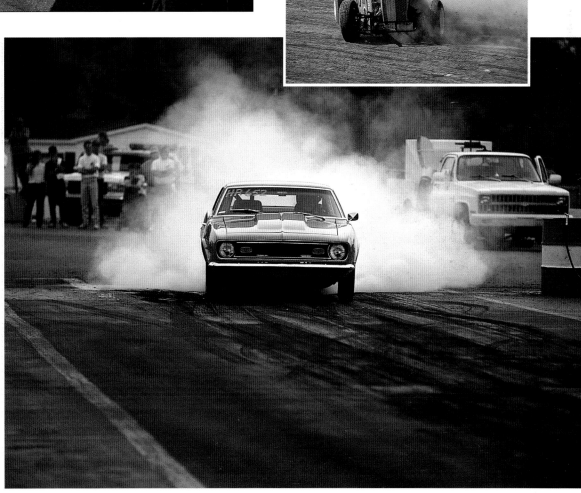

MARCH 1994

"It was a wild mix of musclecars and nostalgia action that made Fastest Street Car racing look under control," said David Freiburger in his coverage of the Goodguys Hot Rod Drags at Sonoma, California's Sears Point Raceway, ending the 1993 drag racing season. The event brings out an eclectic mix of machinery, such as "Hollywood" George Tuers' flamin' 1955 Nomad wheelstander.

APRIL 1994

In the no-foolin' April 1994 issue, in what had become an annual swimsuit spectacular, Steve Coonan photographed Glen Reilly's 1950 Ford. Built by Cecil Proffit, the all-business coupe is 12 inches shorter behind the doors and features a 9-inch roof chop, a 16-inch section job and a 4-inch channel over the rails. To accentuate the already-low car, all pans were rolled and a 1956 Chrysler grille was installed. Poking through the pearl yellow scalloped hood is 490 inches of GMC-blown Chevy.

MAY 1994

While it didn't make the cover, Joe MacPherson's C.A.R.S-constructed 1929 on 1932 rails did take home the nine-foot AMBR trophy from the 1994 Oakland Roadster Show. Styled after early track roadsters, this yellow screamer housed an unusual Infinity Q45 twin-cam V-8 and trans combo. Art and Mike Chrisman also used Infinity independent suspension components mounted on a pair of bobbed 1932 rails, while metal-master Steve Davis massaged all of the sheet metal, Junior Conway squirted 10 gallons of "fly yellow," and Tony Nancy trimmed it in tan Connolly leather.

SEPTEMBER 1994

The cover of the September 1994 issue was a group shot taken at the first-ever *Hot Rod* Magazine Power Festival. Presented by BF Goodrich and sponsored by Dodge, the Power Fest happened at Norwalk Raceway Park in rural Norwalk, Ohio. One of the highlights of the event was the appearance of Troy Trepanier's brand new 1960 Rambler wagon Pro Streeter, dubbed the *Rumblur*. The car was completed mere hours before the show, so it could debut at the first *Hot Rod* Power Fest. In typical Troy form, the *Rumblur* was another Dare to be Different creation supported by a rectangular-tube chassis, ground-hugging stance and an absolutely outstanding engine compartment, featuring a wild Moon cross-ram intake manifold fitted with fuel injection.

NOVEMBER 1994

1994 was definitely the year of the swimsuit, with models appearing in numerous issues, including November, which featured *Hot Rod*'s giveaway 1957. Described as "The *Son of Green Machine*" (*Hot Rod*'s December 1991 project clean n' green 1955 Chevy), this California Street Rods-built 1957 was powered by a Chevy LT1 crate motor with Howell-engineered injection. On a 2,000-mile shakedown run to the site of sister-magazine's second annual Rod & Custom Americruise, *the Son of Green Machine* performed flawlessly and was eventually given away in a reader competition.

JANUARY 1995
In the annals of *Hot Rod* history, few rods can compare with the Fred Warren DuPont *Smoothster*. Designed by Larry Erickson, designer of both the *Aluma Coupe* and *CadZZilla*, the *Smoothster* was original being built for Robbie Midollo by Craig Naff. Unfortunately, for Robbie, he ran out of loot, and the car went to Hot Rods by Boyd, where it was finished for Fred. The 66 grille bars were hand-formed by George Gould before being sanded smooth by Chip Foose, shown here fitting the top with Pete Morrell.

FEBRUARY 1995

Alex Xydias opened one of the first speed shops in the country in 1945. Located, ironically, at 1104 Victory Boulevard in Burbank, California, it was home to the SO-CAL Racing Team which, in the ensuing years, was a dominant force on the dry lakes, drag strips and Bonneville Salt Flats in the early days of the sport. SO-CAL's first effort was this P-38 Lightning tank-bodied lakes special, powered by a Bobby Meeks-built Ford V-8-60. Running on straight methanol, the *Special* ran 130.155 miles per hour at El Mirage in August 1948. It eventually ran over 150 miles per hour with the V-8-60 and 198.340 with a 296-inch Merc V-8. The car was eventually restored for Bruce Meyer by Pete Chapouris' SO-CAL Speed Shop.

MARCH 1995

Like Jim Ewing before him, Jack Chisenhall of Vintage Air had a dream of building a true 200-mile per hour-plus street car wrapped in the body of Raymond Lowey's famous 1953 Studebaker. Unlike Jim, however, Jack intended to run his 200 with the vintage air conditioning on! Using a Mark Stielow-designed NASCAR road race-style chassis and 705 inches of Dart Merlin Superblock capped off with a pair of Big Chief cylinder heads, Jack realized his dream by blasting the Bonneville traps at a sizzling 219 miles per hour.

DECEMBER 1995
A little tire smoke never hurt anyone, especially not Ron Rhodes. When *Hot Rod* staffers first saw the car at the Norwalk, Ohio, *Hot Rod* Power Festival, it looked to be an all show but no go cream puff, so straight were its body panels and so smooth its paint—there were no battle scars. Under the hood, it was even more disarming, with a $3,200 406-inch small-block. Looks, however, can be deceiving, and Ron's $200 initial purchase netted a 11.36 elapsed time at 117 miles per hour.

APRIL 1995
By the mid 1990s, nostalgia more than nitro was the fuel that drove hot rodding, and a portion of *Hot Rod*'s past was the Greer-Black-Prudhomme dragster. The winningest fuel car in the history of drag racing was campaigned 30 years, prior when it pounded the Pomona pavement around 7.7 seconds at speeds around 208 miles per hour and made household names of engine builder Keith Black and driver Don Prudhomme. By 1965, the car was considered obsolete, and Black sold it. It passed through a number of hands before finding a home with metal shaper extraordinaire Steve Davis, who eventually restored it for Bruce Meyer.

JANUARY 1996

As subtle as *CadZZilla* was radical, the newest ride of ZZ Top's Billy F. Gibbons in 1996 was this 1949 Ford coupe. Built by Pete Chapouris' SO-CAL Speed Shop, *Kopperhed* was one of those what-if cars. What if Ford had experimented in 1949 with a three-window version of its venerable business coupe. Jim Jacobs (Jake) was given the task of transforming five holes into three and lengthening the doors ten inches before shoehorning in a 1957 T-Bird motor. *Kopperhed* debuted at a gala party at the newly-opened Petersen Automotive Museum in Los Angeles, California.

FEBRUARY 1996

From the very beginning, *Hot Rod* founder Robert E. Petersen (Pete) staffed his magazine with like-minded enthusiasts who were active in buying, selling, building and driving hot rods. He rightly felt that this hands-on experience generated the right kind of editorial, and in 1960 the team of Wally Parks, Ray Brock, Bob Greene, Racer Brown, Eric Rickman and Tom Medley fielded this 1957 Plymouth Savoy in the 14-day annual NASCAR "speed-a-thon." Prepped by Dean Moon, the 318-inch Fury was canned for a 389-inch Tony Capana motor that produced 448 horses on straight alky. Eventually, with Ray Brock at the wheel, the car ran a best one-way of 183 miles per hour at Bonneville. This replica of the original car was built for Wally Parks by his friends at the NHRA.

SEPTEMBER 1996
Nine days and 2,900 miles of tire smoke was how *Hot Rod* staffers described the 1996 *Hot Rod* Power Tour. Leading the pack out of Los Angles all the way to Mt. Clements, Michigan, was Plymouth's new Prowler—a suitable debut for the then-new aluminum-bodied, V-6-powered production rod. Alongside the Prowler was Dan Jacobs' Troy Trepanier-built 1939 Chevy, *Predator*, which drove all the way from L.A. to Detroit and back to Manteno, Illinois.

MARCH 1997
The lines of the 1955 Ford Thunderbird are regarded by many to be timeless. However, as hot rodders are fond of saying, "Anybody can restore a car, but it takes real guts to cut one up." Nevertheless, that was the desire of Henry and Sandra Aguirre, who had Roy Brizio dissect a pristine example to create their dream car. With updated suspension and a Ford Motorsport SVO EFI 351-inch engine endowed with a SVO PowerDyne blower, this 'Bird really knows how to fly.

APRIL 1997

Still looking for the fastest street cars on the planet, *Hot Rod*'s April 1997 issue featured 23-year-old Landon Jordan's 1969 Camaro. Using a David Wolf-prepared chassis and a 632-inch Donovan block fitted with BME pistons, GRP rods, Erson roller cam and heads ported by Mike Yelvi, Jordan parted the waters in 7.12 seconds at a speed of 195 miles per hour.

OCTOBER 1997

Hot Rod called the story "Buck-Fifty In A Brick, Or How to Run 150 miles per hour Legally at the Pony Express 100." During the 1990s, the trend toward high-speed, on-highway shoot outs on remote roads in Nevada grew in popularity despite a few spills. In 1997, Jeff Smith tried his hand at the Pony Express 100 on a desolate stretch of Highway 350 and did manage a run in excess of 156 miles per hour. Of course, Jeff wasn't the fastest. That honor fell to Rick Doria, whose Corvette hit a top speed of 211 miles per hour on his way to a two-way average of 194.069.

MAY 1997

Designed by Chip Foose and built specifically for the *Hot Rod* Power Tour, this 10-inch-wider-than-stock 1957 Chevy was yet another product of Hot Rods by Boyd. Again, this was a "what if" concept and asked the question, "What if GM had been playing with the 1959 Impala convertible's proportions two years earlier?" Starting with a 1959 Impala cowl and windshield, which was chopped 2 inches, the team at Hot Rods by Boyd spent a scant four months hammering and welding sheets of steel until it resembled a 1957 Chevy—sorta.

AUGUST 1997

Except during the van craze, very few trucks have made the cover of *Hot Rod*. All that changed, however, in August 1997 when the incredibly popular Galaxie 500 truck of Trader's made it in action alongside Rudy Ruano's 1970 1/2 Z28. Designed by Steve Stanford, the Ford F-150-based Galaxie featured hand-painted chrome trim by Stanford and Pete Santini, a full complement of Street Scene Equipment and lowering by Bell Tech.

FEBRUARY 1998

Shown under construction in the December 1997 issue, Troy Trepanier's latest made it between the pages of the February 1998 issue. Built for George Poteet, *The Sniper* was based on a1954 Plymouth Savoy convertible and there, all resemblance ends. Troy developed his own 3x4-inch frame, fitted with 1997 Viper Coupe suspension narrowed to fit. Power also comes from a 1997 Viper V10 motor of 488 cubic inches. Notice we said convertible, but what you see is hardtop. That's because Troy hand-built the roof and windshield pillars and performed numerous other body mods, including installing E320 Mercedes headlights. *Sniper* is but another testament to this young rodder's talents.

JANUARY 1998

To celebrate *Hot Rod*'s 50th anniversary, *Hot Rod* commissioned Chip Foose to design and Roy Brizio to build an update version of the very first cover car from the January 1948 issue. The original car, a 1927 track T owned by Regg Schlemmer, created a stir when it ran 136 miles per hour back in 1947, much the same as the new car did when it was unveiled at the 1997 SEMA Show to celebrate *Hot Rod*'s big five-oh! Using a Brizio-built chassis, Wescott fiberglass body and an Edelbrock-prepped 302-inch Ford, the *Cover Clone*, as it became known, followed the lines of the original, down to its flame paint job. In this case, however, instead of black flames on a yellow field, Art Himsl used *Hot Rod*'s colors of red on white.

HOT ROD Magazine

VOL. 1, NO. 1 • • • PRICE 25c   WORLD'S MOST COMPLETE HOT ROD COVERAGE   JANUARY 1948

HOT ROD OF THE MONTH

Sitting in the driver's seat is Eddie Hulse, who, a few moments after this picture was taken, drove number 668, to set a new SCTA record for Class C roadsters. Hulse, a native Californian, nosed out Randy Shinn, a long-time top honor holder for the RC Class. Shinn's old record was 129.40 in a channeled Mercury T.

Keeping the Car Out Front by George Riley—Page 10

INDEX